Welcome to the

FRONT ROW

A Plea for Equal Access to God in Orthodox Jewish Culture

CHARLES R. KRIVCHER

Book design by CreateSpace

ISBN: 1484811585
ISBN-13: 9781484811580
Library of Congress Control Number: 2013903116
Charles R Krivcher, Nashville, TN

"Once we are old enough to have had an education, the first step toward self-esteem for most of us is not to learn but to unlearn. We need to demystify the forces that have told us what we *should be* before we can value what *we are*. That's difficult enough when we have been misvalued by an upbringing or social bias that is clearly wrong. But what happens when this wrongness is taught as objective truth? When the most respected sources of information make some groups invisible and others invincible?"

– Gloria Steinem
(From *Revolution From Within;
A Book Of Self Esteem,* Little,
Brown & Company, 1992 at page 109)

—————

"I simply want Orthodox Jewish women brought to equal status with Orthodox Jewish men because it is clearly unfair to do anything less. They should be able to choose their own roles and limitations if any."

– Charles R. Krivcher *(2012)*

A lawyer and retired soldier argues that Orthodox Jewish women should be fully included as rabbis, cantors and minyan members.

In this short work, attorney Krivcher, a retired lieutenant colonel in the U.S. Army and a member of a Reform Jewish congregation, pleads for fairness for Orthodox Jewish women, who face religious participation restrictions that Orthodox Jewish men do not. He describes a catalyzing episode after his father's funeral, when mourners decided to form a minyan, or a quorum of members for communal worship. "Soft whispers circulated as heads were counted in a search for the magic formula of ten men....Despite my pleas for flexibility, I was dismissively advised that none of the women present would be counted." He and his wife left rather than support such marginalization. Today, the author attends a Reform temple with a female cantor and assistant rabbi. Krivcher comes by his commitment to fairness via his background in civil rights. To many readers, fairness may seem like a self-evident good, but an Orthodox Jew might ask: What does fairness, or a woman's natural ability, have to do with following God's laws? The body of laws, or halakhah, governing Jewish life might be up for argument, but Krivcher refuses to engage in "biblical or liturgical analysis, as I hope to avoid becoming mired in...

several centuries of interpretation." But to Torah-observant Jews, that's an important discussion, and as a result, Krivcher's plea may fall on deaf ears. Interestingly, the author hardly mentions feminists within Orthodoxy, assuming that most Orthodox women suffer from low self-esteem; instead, he calls on Orthodox men to lead change. He does note that some women are trying to bring about change in the context of halakhah, but again, he has little patience with the subject—to the detriment of achieving his aim. This short work is lengthened some with extras, including the text of a Martin Luther King speech.

A well-intentioned, heartfelt plea for fairness, but one unlikely to change minds.

-Kirkus Reviews

TABLE OF CONTENTS

ACKNOWLEDGMENTS

"Republic, I like the sound of the word. ...It means people can live free, talk free. ... Some words give you a feeling...makes me feel tight in the throat. ...Some words give you a feeling that makes your heart warm. Republic is one of those words."
— John Wayne, portraying Davy Crockett in *The Alamo*, United Artists and Batjac Productions, 1960

M y wife, Ilsa S. Krivcher, has been a patient and supportive editor, exceeding all expectations, often serving as devil's advocate with regard to many of my ideas. In a nutshell, she is the crème de la crème, as my wonderful mother-in-law Nettie Brooks Strauch used to say. For me, she is *it*!

Harriet K. Freiberger, the oldest of my three sisters and an accomplished author herself (*Lucien Maxwell, Villain or Visionary*, Sunstone Press, 1999), has been both a mentor and a continuing source of encouragement. I consider her writing skills and sense of history to be among the very best. My only regret is that she and I are not geographically closer, which as a practical matter would have allowed more time for brainstorming over coffee and each day's sunrise, with the result of a better book.

Nancy Richardson, who, until just recently served our Reform Temple (Congregation Ohabai Sholom in Nashville) as director of membership and programming, also provided some editorial advice at the midpoint of this work. However, more importantly, she has been a perfect sounding board because of her deep knowledge of Torah. She has also pointed me to the Book of Malachi for reference and further suggested that I use the term *gender* as opposed to *sex*. She has also served as a member of our temple's board of trustees.

Our temple's new cantor, Tracy Fishbein, is a continuing and genuine source of inspiration both by virtue of her angelic and gloriously powerful voice, and because her empathy for the subject matter is so genuine. She refreshed my memory with regard to the Book of Proverbs, chapter 31 (the passage on the woman of valor) and introduced me to a few interpretations of it. She reminded me of Reform Judaism's use of the term *egalitarian* to acknowledge the equality of men and women in the evolution of our prayer book over the years. Quite frankly, and to the point of this book, if she had sought employment in an

Orthodox synagogue, her application would have been summarily rejected (simply because of gender), thus denying her an opportunity to stand at the head of her own congregation in this capacity.

Our temple's inspirational rabbi, Shana Goldstein Mackler, could not have been more supportive. She possesses a persuasive leadership style, one which I describe as being characteristic of Reform rabbinic wisdom. Wise beyond her years, she has been careful to point out that as a Reform Jew looking into the world of Orthodoxy, I am an outsider looking in, a notion also echoed by Nancy Richardson and Cantor Fishbein. They are quite correct, and I concur. However, looking again to the point of this book (even from the perspective of an outsider), the thought that Orthodox Judaism, as a matter of policy, would turn away Rabbi Mackler simply because of gender is unacceptable to this writer on grounds of basic and fundamental fairness.

Thus, as a way of honoring Rabbi Mackler and Cantor Fishbein (and making my point at the same time), it is my intention to donate 10 percent of this book's gross proceeds to their respective discretionary funds at the Temple (5 percent to each). These funds are known as "The Rabbi Mackler Discretionary Fund" and "The Cantor Fishbein Discretionary Fund," respectively.

Further, I dedicate this book to the memory of Dr. Martin Luther King Jr., whose leadership of the American civil rights movement has become more meaningful than ever. His short life, characterized by such traits as faith, persistence, and personal courage served to bring this nation together for the purpose of embracing its ethnic diversity. Thanks in large part to his persuasive power, today's America possesses an unusual sense of synergistic strength. This synergy combines generations of culturally diverse immigrants, who more than anything else simply want to be Americans and to live in this land where "everybody gets a shot," as President Barack Obama is fond of saying. It was Dr. King and the civil rights movement that made "We the people" a reality for all Americans. Today's United States of America, this wonderful republic (that word which gave John Wayne such a warm feeling), lives and thrives under the protection of a living constitution. Here is the place where we as individuals have respect for one another as well as for the rule of law (because, as the cliché goes, the rules apply equally to all of us). Indeed, I thank God each day for the blessing of living in this republic. Likewise, as a way to honor Dr. King's memory, it is my intention to donate 5 percent of this book's gross proceeds to The Martin Luther King, Jr. Center for Nonviolent Social Change in Atlanta, Georgia.

Finally, I dedicate this work to the unexpressed feelings of millions of Orthodox Jewish women, who, solely because of gender are denied even the opportunity to be counted in the formation of a minyan.

DEDICATION LETTER

This book is dedicated to my wife, Ilsa Gail Strauch Krivcher, also endearingly referred to by this writer as "Ma Generale," "Mr. Wilson," and sometimes, "Ilsa Gail."

My Dearest Ilsa,

I have loved you since I was fifteen years old. My lover and best friend, we've been sitting together (sometimes on the front row, but always side by side) and praying together as a couple for more than forty-one years, first at Temple Israel in Memphis, Tennessee, and since 1987 in Nashville as members of Congregation Ohabai Sholom.

I could never embrace any rule that would require us to sit apart from each other in services (especially with me front and center and you behind the curtain, in the back or off to the side). When I reflect on the moments we have shared in temple, our whispers of loving support for each other, the shared smiles, a look here, a touch there, perhaps holding hands, sometimes with one's arm around the other's shoulder, and all in God's sanctuary, I am most grateful.

Suffice it to say, I am quite certain that God wholeheartedly approves of such closeness whenever the cantor softly sings "Mi She-Berakh," and we acknowledge the taste of the other's tears. We know these tears as the involuntary demonstration of joy and grief that flow spontaneously with the recall of memories of our parents and others who have come before us, the lives that have been such a blessing to you and me in no small way.

Please know that in my daily prayers, I thank God for you. As ever, with my compliments, respect, and all my love, always,

CRK, Charles, and sometimes
Colonel House

INTRODUCTION

"Remember, no one can make you feel inferior without your consent."
— Eleanor Roosevelt (*From feminist.com / Inspiring Quotes by Women*)

———•———

Written from the heart, and holding nothing back, this book is about dignity. It is about the inner strength and personal courage that will be necessary for Orthodox Jewish women to achieve spiritual equality with Orthodox Jewish men. It is about pride, self-esteem, and self-respect. It is not a work of biblical or liturgical analysis, as I hope to avoid becoming mired in what has already become several centuries of interpretation (this scholar said this and that scholar wrote something else). It is rather, a short book that speaks from the gut and sounds a call to action for millions of Orthodox Jewish women in America and around the globe. It also recognizes that Orthodox rabbis will need the courage to look squarely into their respective mirrors for the wisdom to understand that the reflections contained therein represent the entities most responsible for making things right. For these rabbis and for all Orthodox Jewish men, it is about their ability to change. Such change will require extraordinary courage. By their reaching out to bring real dignity to women, they will also make their own lives a blessing, a lofty goal to which we as Jews always aspire.

It is a work about freedom, equality, and transformation, a work that asks genuine questions: What does it really mean to say that we are all equal in the eyes of God? What does it mean for women to enjoy equal protection under God's law or to have equal access to God? How might it feel for any Orthodox Jewish woman to look into the eyes of her rabbi, her husband, or her male significant other and respectfully insist on his acknowledgment that men and women are equals in every regard? When she is set apart or denied participation to allegedly protect her from something, is she in receipt of respect? Or is she being demeaned by virtue of the fact that she has no choice and must be kept in her place? How much individual courage is required for an Orthodox woman to organize a group within her synagogue, dedicated to the proposition that the rabbi must take a leadership role in championing her natural and unalienable right to be absolutely equal to any Orthodox Jewish man? What is an unalienable right? Can such rights be unilaterally infringed upon or marginalized by men? How is she to overcome patronizing objections that have been steeped in centuries of Orthodox tradition? How can she pull her Orthodox male counterpart out of his comfort zone to see her side of the equation? What will it take to shock the conscience of Orthodox Judaism over its treatment of women?

More questions come to mind: Is it even possible to imagine that an Orthodox Jewish woman might become president of the United States of America, yet be unable to be counted in the formation of a minyan, serve as an Orthodox rabbi or cantor, or be granted access to the front row of the synagogue during services? Why must every Orthodox Jewish woman understand that good self-esteem is the key to achieving equal status with men? What could Orthodox Jewish women learn from Dr. Martin Luther King Jr. and his leadership role within the American civil rights movement or from Gloria Steinem? Can Orthodox Jewish women find Rosa Parks's courage and determination to be treated equally? How do women muster this kind of courage in order to prevail? How will Orthodox rabbis rationalize their efforts to throw out the old paradigms? Finally, does God specifically require that today's Orthodox woman take a back seat to her male counterpart or to become invisible? Current Orthodoxy would say yes. I say no and offer the entire subject matter for open review by the widest possible Jewish audience.

Initially, it was not my intention to write a book. What began as a personal evolution of prayer emerged as a passionate effort to transform some of the basic cultural tenets of Orthodox Judaism. I have relied largely on personal experiences as a way to introduce some of the key inequities plaguing millions of Orthodox Jewish women. Then, unlike many such discussions, I have attempted to offer sound rationale as to why such discriminatory practices are patently unfair. Further, my proposal to fix the problem suggests that two sets of dynamics must occur. First, Orthodox rabbis must assume a leadership role for change. Second, Orthodox Jewish women must harness the same power used by African Americans during the civil rights movement to recover and assert both their individual and collective self-esteem.

The reader who peruses this introduction is likely to ask, why now? Why this subject? The easy answer relative to time is that in my state of retirement, I am finally free of the practical constraints that might affect my ability to speak out. This is indeed a wonderful feeling and a firm platform on which to write. With regard to the subject matter, perhaps it is simply my naïve expectation that in God's eyes we are all of equal value and, as such, entitled to a level playing field.

As an admission, the reader will observe that because I am a lawyer and retired soldier, my approach to resolving any issue is fair minded and straightforward to a fault. My training as a career military intelligence officer drives me to perform the necessary objective analysis, recognize the deficiencies in a given situation, and then to promptly take decisive corrective action. Thus, it is not surprising that this book demands an immediate departure from Orthodoxy's status quo toward women, consensually and persuasively if possible, but immediately nonetheless.

As a caveat of sorts, I have been personally reminded by Dr. Wendy Zierler, associate professor of modern Jewish literature and feminist studies at the Hebrew Union College's Jewish Institute of Religion, that "the struggle to bring Orthodoxy into alignment with feminism is an evolutionary process, and one that needs to be undertaken within the Orthodox community as it depends on issues of Jewish law (halakhah) and practice that are not operative in the same way in Reform Judaism." Generally speaking, I concur with her reasoning and wish only that the evolution should proceed at a faster pace. Tomorrow morning would be soon enough.

Why not now? Who is to be injured if a woman's soul is brought to equal status with the soul of any man? What is the downside? Indeed, some "evolutionary progress" has been made in the last several hundred years. However, the incremental baby steps toward equality are microscopic allowances by a male-controlled, religious hierarchy and as such, seem meaningless when evaluated against the strategic goal of achieving real and genuine equality. In battle, it is like celebrating an enemy's body count when the strategic objective has yet to be reached. Are we to wait another year, ten years, fifty years, or several hundred years for this hierarchy to "evolve" and to grant precious inches of microscopic advance when there are miles to travel? How many generations of women must remain invisible when minyans are formed while Orthodoxy's men chew the issues and decide what they will allow relative to change? Where would these men obtain such power?

My patience is thin when it comes to ending discrimination, overreaching, and oppression. Time is of the essence and every day which passes without change is wasted. After all, in the end, we are not just kicking around ideas about observance. We are dealing with real people with real souls who are compelled (without choice and without a say in the matter) to travel through a lifetime without equality. Suffice it to say, for me this issue is both compelling and personal.

It is imperative for the reader to appreciate that my passion for equality is driven by a powerful and overriding sense of "justice for all" (as we declare in our Pledge of Allegiance), a universal, natural justice that God will always favor with divine approval under any objective analysis. If indeed our charge is to "walk humbly" with our God then is it also imperative that women be required to walk humbly behind their male counterparts? My intention is simply to suggest that in the eyes of God, *equal* should mean equal under every set of circumstances.

This book is my effort to level the playing field for Orthodox Jewish women by offering clear and convincing evidence in support of a necessary cultural transformation. For example, this change-over must provide that every woman possesses the freedom and the power to choose whether or not she would like to become an ordained Orthodox rabbi or cantor. Simply stated, the decision must necessarily be based on her individual interests, her character, and the merits of her application—not upon the arbitrary decision of male-controlled Orthodoxy, which seems to decree that she is not allowed that choice solely because of gender. Such decrees always seem to be supported by any number of faulty rationalizations, interpretations, and male insights into God's current intentions.

My repeated question for Orthodoxy's rule makers is this: how can you be absolutely certain that God's current intention is to deny this choice to women? After all, the stakes are quite high, quite significant. My objective in this book is to demonstrate the fault lines that run through such arbitrary rulemaking. I feel compelled to tell a convincing story, one that will bring about real discussion and immediate change.

As a member of the Nashville Bar Association, I attended the 2012 Law Day luncheon, where the featured speaker was US Senator Lamar Alexander of Tennessee. Opening his address, he referenced some advice from his longtime friend, author, and fellow Tennessean Alex Haley, who died in 1992. As an aside, those who know Alexander also know that he likes to quote his friend Haley and always presents his audience with a smile when he does so. Alexander recalled that Alex once told him that if he would begin his speeches by saying, "Let me tell you a story," his audience would listen more closely.

In this book I also want to tell you a story as a way of establishing credibility. This centuries-old issue is examined from my perspective as a sixty-three –year-old Reform Jew living in Tennessee. My objective has been to use my legal and military experiences to complement my passion for equal protection of natural rights under God's law. Simply stated, it is my hope that the reader will appreciate not having some old soldier, who happens to be a Reform Jew and a Tennessee lawyer, to simply open up with his demand for centuries of historical practice to change, without at least some autobiographical support.

I was particularly moved by former Secretary of State Hillary R. Clinton's March 12, 2012, remarks to the Women of the World conference: "Why extremists always focus on women remains a mystery to me. But they all seem to. It doesn't matter what country they're in or what religion they claim. They want to control women. They want to control how we dress. They want to control how we act." She continued, "The United States needs to set an example for the entire world and reject efforts to marginalize any of us."

She was, of course, quite correct, and the question for Orthodox Jewish men is whether they possess the emotional wherewithal to bring women voluntarily to equal status before they themselves are considered to be extremists of a sort, before they are judged to be something other than the well-intentioned pious Jews that they strive to be. Orthodox Jewish men must simply act to relinquish their power over women, and Orthodox rabbis will have to lead the way forward.

Quite candidly, as long as women are forbidden to become either Orthodox rabbis or cantors, until they can be counted in the formation of a minyan or occupy an equal number of front-row seats in synagogue during services (and in dress of her choosing), Orthodox Jewish men will sense their weakness, their continued acquiescence in being substantively powerless. The result of this dynamic of acquiescence is that such men will retain both an implied and apparent authority to continue overreaching women. Would this not be marginalizing them, as Secretary Clinton has suggested? Of course, the rhetorical answer is yes.

Most recently, I found renewed inspiration from the words of Elie Wiesel in his widely acclaimed book *Night,* originally published in 1958 by Les Editions de Minuit and converted into an audio book by Recorded Books, LLC, in 2006. Narrated by George Guidall, this insightful and compelling account of young Elie's experience during the Holocaust needs no introduction. I listened intently to the horrors associated with the physical and psychological processes of exclusion. The Nazis used these processes to marginalize, then to control, and finally to exterminate so many millions of Jews simply because they were Jews. In early 1933 the Nazis immediately relegated the Jews to a position of invisibility.

It is absolutely shocking that Orthodox Jewish men who lived through the Holocaust, as well as their successors today, think nothing of gently yet purposefully demanding that Orthodox Jewish women be treated as marginalized invisibles (my term) when it comes to substantive religious matters. It is extremely disconcerting that Orthodox Jewish men decree with absolute certainty in the correctness of their decision making, that no woman can become a rabbi or cantor, etc., etc., etc. The implied arrogance of this marginalization is overwhelming to me as a human being, and quite frankly, it must change. It is interesting that Mr. Wiesel began to question all the rules and religious boundaries during his terrifying experience in the death camps. *Welcome to the Front Row* plainly demands that Orthodox Jewish men and rabbis in particular, question the traditional religious rules and boundaries that marginalize Orthodox Jewish women, keeping them as invisible participants before God.

My feeling is that readers will appreciate the straightforward logic of Dr. Thomas Childers, professor of history at the University of Pennsylvania, as he introduces and then concludes his lecture series *A History of Hitler's Empire.*[1] It is powerful and even disconcerting to find support for the liberation of Orthodox Jewish women in a lecture series designed to summarize the rise and fall of an empire that singled out Jews for extermination, simply because of their religion. Professor Childers's approach is logical and should raise serious questions for Orthodoxy's rule makers with

---

1   2nd ed., the Teaching Company Limited Partnership, 2001.

regard to decreeing arbitrary restrictions upon women simply because of gender. He explains that as a general rule, a totalitarian regime is absolutely certain that it alone is in possession of all of the answers to the big questions and there is no appeal from its official decisions or decision-making processes.

As a Jew, it hurts me to even hint at such comparisons, yet I do so only because Orthodoxy's rule makers seem intent on maintaining their casual and dismissive attitude in response to substantive questions about women's rights in relation to God. Quite frankly, and somewhat sarcastically, I observe that such practices have served to keep women firmly fixed in their place and under paternalistic control. What will be required to shock the conscience of Orthodoxy's rule makers? I feel like Moses talking to Pharaoh as he demanded, "Let my people go!" In working to understand such questioning of tradition, Dr. Childers might say to start with a blank sheet of paper, to "forget what you know," and to think critically about the denial of rights affected by such Orthodox decision making.

Lastly, how can Orthodox Jewish men be absolutely certain that God has not modernized divine oversight to keep pace with human development? How can they be certain beyond any reasonable doubt that the rules must remain unchanged?

Indeed, if their confidence level is less than 100 percent, say, perhaps 98 percent or 90 percent or less, why not open the door for more inclusive participation by women? Who is to be harmed by more inclusion? What, if any, are the risks involved if the door is opened for inclusionary change?

Reform and Conservative movements seem to be enjoying the fruits of such change, where women are offered dignity and the freedom to "be all they can to be" (paraphrasing the former advertising slogan of the US Army). From the observation of this writer, these fruits are evident in the appearance of happy, smiling, independent, self-assured women, many of whom serve as rabbis, cantors, and presidents of their temples and synagogues. Fully incorporated into the infrastructure of Jewish life, these women enter their temples and synagogues with a sense of dignity and enhanced self-esteem characterized by their heads held high with shoulders back, generally exuding a sense of presence. They do not need antiquated and paternalistic rules of protection to take equal ownership of or to assume equal responsibility for all that is Jewish, both procedurally and substantively.

In other words, these women enter their respective houses of worship just as men would, all of them with the same procedural access to God and all with the same strength of conviction that their prayers are heard in exactly the same way as those uttered by men. Further, just like their male counterparts, they dress as they choose, sit where they please, and aspire to any leadership role that they feel is appropriate for them. And, finally, just as is the case with men (from a purely spiritual standpoint), there is no sense of pretentiousness, arrogance, or superiority that detracts from their shared sense of humility and fervent desire to walk humbly with God. This book challenges Orthodox Jewish men to defend logically, before God's judgment, a set of rules that orders that the soul of one Jew should be counted in order to form a minyan and another discounted, discarded, or simply made invisible because of gender.

Again, it is worth reiterating that my objective here is not to be obnoxiously confrontational to my Orthodox Jewish brothers on this issue of women's equality. I simply want Orthodox Jewish women brought to equal status with Orthodox Jewish men because it is clearly unfair do otherwise and because they should be able to choose their own roles and limitations, if any. When I consider the tremendous value and sense of enrichment brought to our Reform temple by Rabbi Shana Goldstein Mackler and Cantor Tracy Fishbein, I am hard pressed to even imagine how Orthodoxy might rationalize a policy that denies such worthy and wonderful women the right to fulfill their dreams and to be of service simply because of gender. Would it not be more egalitarian, and indeed more equitable, for Orthodoxy to judge them on their respective skill, education, and merit as opposed to excluding them categorically on the sole basis of gender? Would Orthodox men feel the same if they were made invisible by larger society based on their religion? Of course not, and we would call this discrimination or, worse, anti-Semitism.

Most assuredly, Rabbi Mackler will someday have her own congregation as a senior rabbi. Cantor Fishbein has every reason to believe that if she desires to remain as cantor of our temple in Nashville, she will be allowed to do so with great appreciation from the entire congregation. The thought of their respective leadership roles makes me very proud, and in my judgment, serves to make God very proud as well.

Charles R. Krivcher
Nashville, Tennessee
March 14, 2013

CHAPTER 1...THIS IS AMERICA, THE PROMISE LAND

"Son, you must be good to the girls; respect them as your equals in every way," and "say your prayers every day."

— Abe Krivcher, 1950s

———

While God may have given the first Ten Commandments to Moses on Mount Sinai, it was my father, Abe Krivcher, who prescribed the following two commandments for my personal use at a very early age: "Son, you must be good to the girls; respect them as your equals in every way," and "say your prayers every day." Before his death in 1997, I wondered whether he sensed the profound impact of such simple instructions. Now, more than fifteen years since his death, I am quite certain that he absolutely knew the future value of those words as he spoke from the heart, from his considerable personal experience with the women in our family. He was, after all, married to my wonderful mother and was well underway in raising my three older sisters when I entered the world in 1949. The words produced immediate benefits to us both, yet in a larger sense, their potential to grow from tiny seeds of advice into mature thought processes fit precisely into his long-term strategy for my personal development.

As early as my elementary school years, I incorporated his instructions into a set of principles that later matured into core building blocks of my value system, one that I like to think is guided by a moral compass of sorts. However, it was by accident that my commitment to respect women as equals and to say my prayers every day would coalesce in a way that raised troubling questions about the treatment of Orthodox Jewish women at the hands of Orthodox Jewish men. Even at a young age and without much understanding of Torah, it was my sense of things that Orthodox Jewish women seemed to know their place (so to speak). It was also my observation that as long as they lived their lives as expected, harmony could prevail. However, questioning the rules was not encouraged.

Whether such treatment is intentional or otherwise, the paradigm must change, and in a way that brings Orthodox Judaism into the twenty-first century on two critical issues. First is a required acquiescence on the part of Orthodox Jewish rabbis that women should be counted exactly the same as men when forming a minyan (much like having the right to vote). The cloak of invisibility must be thrown off; they must be counted, period, nonnegotiable. Second, their ability to serve as rabbis or cantors and their seating in religious services must be made equal as well. In short, they must be welcomed to the front row, as equal participants, in the clothing of their own choosing, with no strings attached.

My feelings on this subject did not take shape overnight, but rather had their origin in the cultural dynamics of my childhood. How interesting it was to be a boy with three older sisters. Considering the family as a whole, we were the quintessential American, Southern, classical Reform Jewish family in Memphis. Actually, my mother, Marie Cohen Krivcher, and father steered the family's course as hard-working, good-spirited co-captains, each having full authority to make any decision. Their ability to guide the family with two steering wheels while speaking with one voice was practicable only because their relationship was characterized by love and mutual respect. They led persuasively and by example, demonstrating with every decision-making process that as partners, as husband and wife, they were equals in every way. Each worked to enhance the other's self-esteem as well as that of the children. The result was a nurturing environment of positive reinforcement and a feeling that nothing limited my dreams or those of my sisters. Household tasks were considered as unisex, and the entire family worked, played, and prayed together.

The family's egalitarian commitment to virtually everything was consistent with all we knew as American Reform Jews. In the mid-1960s, my grandfather, Joseph Krivcher (a Ukrainian immigrant), reminded me that an important part of my being a Reform Jew was simply to be the best possible American citizen, thankful every day for God's blessing that allowed us to live in this wonderful place called America.

Grandpa Krivcher had left many of the old ways back in Russia. While he respected the right of Orthodox Judaism to follow dietary laws, establish restrictive female dress codes, require separate seating in services, and preclude women from becoming rabbis or cantors or being counted in order to form a minyan, he had little use for such traditions in modern-day America. Often he would exclaim with genuine excitement, "This is America, the promise land!" He learned to speak perfect English and was quick to tell anyone that, while Israel would always be a homeland and refuge worthy of every Jew's support, our precious United States of America is the place to have a home. For him, the United States was the greatest place on the planet, and to this end he encouraged the entire family to become fully integrated into America's culture. He was certain that the days of building walls and living in ghettos were gone forever and becoming good Americans would only serve to enhance our faith as Jews. He encouraged me to join the armed forces of the United States as a way to do my part, to say "thank you" for the blessings of freedom God and our Constitution had given us.

In 1926 he secured a family membership at Temple Israel in Memphis. He later served on its board of trustees, as did both of my parents. Grandpa Joe and my dad were also life members of B'nai B'rith.

Our beloved Temple Israel was at the center of our religious and social lives, and the congregation was blessed with an unbroken string of dynamic Reform Jewish rabbis. Men and women sat together in services as their prayers were offered primarily in English, firm in the belief that the offering language was largely irrelevant as long as prayerful communication was sincere and well intentioned. Confirmation was for boys and girls alike as we moved together toward religious maturity, and in religious school we were taught that women could form a minyan with or without men.

My parents cemented into my head the principle that boys and girls, men and women were equals in every regard. Again speaking from experience, my dad cautioned me on many occasions that if I should ultimately fall in love with an Orthodox Jewish girl, I would be marrying into a very different culture, one characterized by an obsessive compliance with the procedures of religious practice.

CHAPTER 2...THE SUBSTANCE OF REFORM VS. ORTHODOXY'S RULES

"Looking back, I am enormously proud that Reform Jews, led by great American rabbis, acted with honor and with full understanding of the fact that discrimination against any minority represented a loss of civil rights for all of us."

– Charles R. Krivcher, 2012

———

The experience of my teenage years led me to first conclude that thousands of years after the writings contained in the Book of Deuteronomy, God would find it unnecessary to expect strict adherence to many of the practices followed by my Orthodox friends. Chief among these were requirements that placed women either in the back or off to the side of the sanctuary during services. Similarly, it was my observation that females never served as rabbis or cantors and rarely carried the Torah. At day's end on Yom Kippur, almost no females were found in the Orthodox services because, as women, they were expected to prepare the Break Fast meal. For me, this served to create an impression that Orthodox males considered themselves as inherently more important simply because of their gender.

It was not just the work, but rather, it was my observation that, as women, they had no choice in the matter. They were unable to propose to their families that perhaps, on alternating years, roles might be reversed, thus allowing women to remain in services until the end of the day while the males in their lives (older men leading younger ones by example) would excuse themselves to prepare the Break Fast. More distressing still was the fact that women seemed invisible when it came to making other substantive decisions, such as who could be counted for the purpose of forming a minyan (more on this later). Thus, using the example set by my parents and my reform temple, I resolved to embrace something completely different in the development of my relationship with God. My relationship would focus on substance, on making the world a better place for all of us.

For Rabbi James A. Wax, who guided Temple Israel through the turbulence of the 1950s and 1960s, social justice was the paramount order of the day. He understood the urgency of the work to be done and knew that our reform congregation could never treat women as second class on the one hand and march in support of civil rights for African Americans and other minorities on the other. He acted as a mentor for his successor, Rabbi Harry K. Danziger, who in the 1960s served as assistant rabbi and later assumed the post of senior rabbi at Temple Israel in 1978 with Rabbi Wax's retirement. Steeped in the same Classical Reform tradition, Rabbi Danziger likewise served with distinction and presently holds the position of rabbi emeritus at Temple Israel and has served as a past president of the Central Conference of American Rabbis.

Thus, with this snapshot of my family's Southern Reform orientation, we can now look to my evolution of prayer and its collision course with the treatment of women in Orthodoxy. The early 1950s brought my first experience. My father would come to my room each evening, and right out of *The Union Prayer Book for Jewish Worship*,[2] we would begin with the She' ma and continue with Moses' admonishment in Deuteronomy, "Thou shalt love the Lord, thy God, with all thy heart, with all thy soul, and with all thy might." Happily, reinforced by my studies at the temple's religious school, memorization came with relative ease. Of course, it was also helpful that I was instructed to

---

2   Rev. ed., 1924, the Central Conference of American Rabbis.

always appreciate the real meaning of prayer, to pray with sincerity, and to hold nothing back from God.

It was fashionable in the 1950s for Reform Jewish families in Memphis to send their sons to one of the city's best private elementary schools for boys, Presbyterian Day School (PDS). My parents enrolled me at the earliest opportunity for one primary reason: my three older sisters, who routinely accepted me as their charge for after-school care, were limited in their appreciation of my zest for football, baseball, toy soldiers, and so on. At PDS I received my first dose of comparative religious study. Indeed, prayer began to look different from our practice at Temple Israel's Sunday school, which I attended with absolute regularity from kindergarten through post confirmation.

As a member of the PDS boys' choir and as a participant in the school's religion classes, I welcomed the comparative religious experience. In most instances it was easy to distinguish the Christian liturgy from my Reform Jewish beliefs, simply by substituting *God* for *Jesus* in the various hymns and readings. The school insisted on mutual respect and, as such, Rabbi Wax was a regular speaker. He knew the value of creating positive Jewish impressions. Besides, the school sanctuary's gigantic pipe organ was very much like the one at Temple Israel. I was beginning to understand that we all worshipped the same God and that prayer was a universal practice, notwithstanding our varying religious traditions. Suffice it to say, respect along with a quest for understanding each person's religious practices were the orders for each day. Rabbi Danziger would continue this tradition in many school settings in the Memphis area.

The early 1960s were watershed years for Memphis, the South, and the United States, as heroes of the civil rights movement led a determined struggle against the forces of racial segregation. One hundred years after the Emancipation Proclamation, the country was finally beginning to embrace its diversity. "We the people" were finally beginning to see ourselves functioning beneath an enormous constitutional umbrella, under which there was room for all Americans from every religion (or no religion at all), each of whom was entitled to equal protection under the law. Rabbi Wax, the temple, and my family were squarely at the center of these issues. Especially in the South, we felt the changes firsthand. Looking back, I am enormously proud that Reform Jews, led by great American rabbis, acted with honor and with full understanding of the fact that discrimination against any minority was a loss of civil rights for all of us. For me, Orthodox Jewish women seemed a logical extension of the word *minority*, and I wondered, even at an early age, why no one stood up for them.

The 1960s also introduced us to a place called Vietnam, for whose struggle more than fifty-eight thousand Americans would give their lives. Hundreds of thousands more would sustain injuries as a result, all of which I mention as an historical backdrop to reinforce the complicated dynamics of American society in the 1960s and early 1970s. Each of us who has lived through this era can tell his or her story. My point is that any struggle for change does not occur in a vacuum.

As an aside and as an acknowledgment of the importance of history, previous generations struggled with change during times characterized by other catastrophic events in history, events such as the Civil War, the Korean War, World War II, the Great Depression, World War I, and the world of racial hatred, within which lynch mobs and Jim Crow terrorized millions of Americans simply because of the color of their skin.

This being said, I suppose it was during this time as well as in the early 1970s that I began to sense with reasonable certainty that Orthodox Jewish women were being denied their equitable religious footing. More than anything else, I think it was the dynamics of the Orthodox Synagogue that left such distinct and negative impressions of how women were considered and treated by their male Orthodox counterparts. My feelings were more the product of my gut than anything else.

From 1971 forward, I had the extremely good fortune to become the son-in-law of a fabulous man, Morris L. Strauch, known affectionately as "Scoby." Ma Generale's father was an absolute prince of a fellow. A Harvard-educated lawyer, former army officer, partner in a prestigious Memphis law firm, life member of Bnai B'rith (former district president and so on), and Orthodox by background, he maintained his membership in Baron Hirsch Synagogue in Memphis concurrent with his membership in Temple Israel. He knew that his family would be more content in a Reform environment, and indeed they were in every regard. I had many occasions to accompany him to services at Baron Hirsch as well as to visit the synagogue for various services, celebrations, and so on, over the years.

It has always been my goal to understand the dynamics of any sanctuary, any house of God (regardless of religion) in an attempt to feel God's presence and to observe the congregants as they pray, move about, and interact with each other. In the Orthodox environment, women became especially noteworthy. "People watching" in this setting and the dynamics of their interactions was very unsettling. It created distinct impressions of inequality, of class structure, of subservience.

I wondered why women sat off to the side or in the back; why many of the women seemed disengaged from the services, simply talking between themselves as opposed to following the service; why they all seemed to accept the responsibility of caring for their young children while their husbands prayed intently, focused on the service. I wondered why all the kitchen activities, help with meals, and other such labor intensive activities were theirs alone. I wondered why there were no female rabbis or cantors. Most importantly, these women seemed weary, beaten down from so much work, so many responsibilities, and so little support from the men in their lives.

Of course, there were exceptions to this observation. The extremely wealthy Orthodox families could afford to have Shabbat homes near the synagogue. They had housekeepers and nannies for children and grandchildren. It was obviously easier for them to maintain kosher homes without the necessity of having to cook, clean, and take care of kids. Unfortunately, these women, these families, were often looked upon as being more pious, more observant, simply because they possessed the wherewithal to afford a luxurious Orthodox lifestyle. All of this seemed to suggest a sort of caste system, with the wealthiest men on top followed closely by the wealthiest women and members of their families. Again, I offer only more observations from my gut.

On the other hand, my general observation of the men left impressions of power, of self-importance. After all, they were front and center in the sanctuary. The rabbis were men as were the cantor and president of the synagogue. Males were clearly in charge. It was not so much that women performed all of the infrastructure work of the family or that they remained invisible behind the curtain in services. Rather, it was the fact (at least from my observation) that they had no choice in the matter in relation to their level of participation. I found this to be very sad and indeed so different from what occurred in my home and at my Reform temple. These women were without any way out. They possessed no right to appeal and, in short, no one was listening. They simply pressed on dutifully, putting one foot in front of the other, always careful not to rock the boat with challenges or complaints of any sort.

Allow me to regress slightly and step back into the sixties. My mother, who suffered from diabetes, was by all accounts (including my own) the kindest, most gentle woman imaginable. Sadly, in early November 1965 (as the first American soldiers were fighting in the Ia Drang Valley of Vietnam's Central Highlands), she asked that I drive her to the doctor. Danger seemed to be at hand,

and unbelievably, she was gone in six weeks, notwithstanding my most humble prayers for her recovery (a separate story altogether).

During those trying days (Winston Churchill
may have said, "those stern days"), my dad sought
the comfort of early-morning services (Shacharit)
offered by Memphis's largest Orthodox synagogue,
Baron Hirsch. He not only liked the schedule and
the group prayers, but also appreciated the warm
welcome extended to him by the synagogue's assistant rabbi and cantor, David W. Skopp. During
my mother's illness and for several weeks after
her death, dad would quietly reflect on his positive experiences at the synagogue. Suffice it to say,
he was quite swept away with the synagogue's
warmth. Yet, for all the convenience of worship
and the relationship he developed with Rabbi
Skopp, he knew very well that my sisters could
never be equal beneficiaries of such experiences
because of their gender. So he made a conscious
choice not to lead the family into a second congregational relationship with the Orthodox synagogue. His daughters were "everything" to him,
and there was simply no way he would usher them
into an environment where they could not stand
on an even playing field with any man. Indeed, as
regarded women and his daughters in particular,
his egalitarian feelings were held to be nearly constitutional in nature.

Now, writing this book, and having the absolute power of hindsight, I am certain that my dad was a de facto Jewish feminist, because as the women in his life matured he would never allow any man or group of men to inhibit their dreams or to treat them as less than absolute equals in every way. No man would tell any of his daughters that she could not become a rabbi or cantor, refuse her a seat front and center at services, or relegate her to invisible status when it came time to form a minyan. My father was straightforward in this regard. He simply prayed for the strength and understanding that would enable him to be as close to God as possible. With little time for the politics of religious dynamics, he was distrustful of anyone or any institution promulgating too many rules or obstacles to impede his efforts.

CHAPTER 3...MY ROOTS AS A JEWISH FEMINIST

"Dozens of black-hatted men jeer and physically accost the girls almost daily, claiming that their very presence is a provocation."
    – Aaron Heller, the Associated Press, 2011

M y dad lived to be eighty-four years of age. Unfortunately, and perhaps, ironically, this wonderful man, who had given me such sage advice as a child and mentored me as a young adult, was unable to know that my full appreciation for the principles of Jewish feminism would begin in earnest on the day of his funeral. Late in the afternoon, after graveside services, most nonfamily mourners had departed. Those of us remaining decided to form a minyan in anticipation of a brief Shiva service. Because we were gathered in a familiar Orthodox home, soft whispers circulated as heads were counted in a search for the magic formula of ten men. I pointed out that we had more than ten willing souls, and given the exigency of the situation, suggested that we proceed. However, with clear disregard for my suggestion, the whispery conversations continued and despite my pleas for flexibility, I was dismissively advised that none of the women present would be counted to form the minyan.

This was extremely disappointing, as it became obvious that women were simply invisible in the eyes of our Orthodox hosts. When a tenth male was finally found, the females were invited by smiling men to join in the service, which of course made the gesture all the more demeaning and patronizing for these modern Jewish women. Personally offended and comfortable in the belief that God would never sanction such inequitable treatment, my wife and I simply left and did not participate. I sensed the humiliation that these women must have felt, especially my wife. How outrageous it was that this wonderful, educated woman, the love of my life, partner in every endeavor, trusted friend, lover, confidant, and mother of our children could be slighted by a small group of men. Were these men acting as God's personal assistants? Were they in receipt of special instructions from God? They were so smug in their religious assessment, so 100 percent certain of procedural correctness, and from all of this they seemed to exude a sense of inflexible arrogance, served by a conclusive presumption of the authority they wielded to ensure the invisibility of every woman in the home.

Subsequently, all manner of scenarios have spun through my head. Indulge the simplicity of a situation in which ten Orthodox Jewish women on a retreat/camping trip in the Colorado's Rocky Mountains are overcome by a sincere desire to form a minyan (several times each day) to offer prayers of thanksgiving for God's wondrous creation. As an aside, if you have ever visited the Rockies, this is very easy to imagine, as the beauty is so overwhelming. Would Orthodoxy insist that these women are so devoid of merit or status to be denied group access to God simply because ten men are absent from the scene? As my four-year-old grandson might observe, "Pops, that would beeeeee ridiculous." Of course, such thinking would be ridiculous and illogical at best, stiff necked and arrogant at worst."

Moreover, if Orthodox Jewish men can even rationalize that these women are not entitled to form a minyan or that they should not have been in the mountains in the first place, please consider the element of control these men have over women. Where is a woman's free will? Where is her right to control her relationships with other women, or with God? Such control has the feel of involuntary servitude, because the women are trapped without a voice; they are simply dismissed. Consider further that if God intended for men to exercise this sort of religious control over women, to deny them the power to pray as a group (with equal effectiveness as men), then perhaps all that we stand for as a nation and a republic are for naught. Can an American Orthodox Jewish man logically hold a copy of our Declaration of Independence, our Constitution, our evolved commitment to the principles of equity and equal protection for everyone in one hand and at the same time embrace centuries of dominant religious control over the hearts and minds of women in the other? I think not, and more importantly, I am nearly certain that God thinks not as well.

The minyan experience remains a moving trigger point in my personal evolution of prayer and reinforces my commitment to embrace the conscience of Jewish feminism. There is something inherently unfair and fundamentally wrong with a male Orthodox hierarchy which controls, sponsors, and validates the treatment of women as second class, or worse. Who are these men and from where could they obtain the power to declare one soul as substandard to another? Such orders do not issue from God's pen. Just imagine that in our America, in 2012, an Orthodox Jewish woman could be president of the United States (arguably the most powerful woman in the world), yet be unable to serve as an Orthodox cantor or rabbi, form a minyan, or sit front and center in an Orthodox service. Such inconsistencies are not only egregiously unfair, they take on characteristics of arrogance, as I have mentioned before. How does the rest of the world observe this inequality? How do Orthodox Jewish men feel about themselves in this analysis?

One logical follow-up question is, should we expect Israel to assume a leadership role in this struggle for change? I think not, as the Israeli government appears to lack the democratic wherewithal to stop such behavior. Unfortunately, Israel has no written constitution with which to guarantee equal protection under the law. Without such a document, which must be treated as the supreme law of the land, and despite some judicial inroads, the road to equality is rather hard going.

While it is safe to say that Israel affects all of us as Jews, the stories of unequal treatment of women in Israel simply pour from every news source. The story of Tanya Rosenblit, serves as one example.[3] Ms. Rosenblit, a journalist traveling in Israel, refused to move to the back of the bus at the insistence of ultra-Orthodox men in the town of

---

3   Abraham Rabinovich, [Like Rosa Parks, Tanya won't bow down to discrimination by giving up her seat on the bus], *The Australian,* December 24, 2011.

Ashdod. A serious civil disturbance was narrowly avoided. A second story involved an eight-year-old schoolgirl, Naama Margolese, who had become a long-term victim of bullying from ultra-Orthodox males who spat on her and called her a whore for dressing "immodestly."[4] This second story describes a scene: "Dozens of black-hatted men jeer and physically accost the girls almost daily, claiming that their very presence is a provocation." Again, how patronizingly ridiculous this is! This writer is aware of neither public apologies nor assurances from the offending parties that such behavior would not be repeated.

In the twenty-first century, does immodest dress or no dress at all make a woman any less valuable or less holy in the eyes of God? Is Erin Stern, the International Federation of Bodybuilders Figure Pro, Ms. Figure Olympia, spokesmodel, and fitness expert, any less Jewish, any less respectful of the Ten Commandments or less committed to the principles of social justice simply because she has developed a beautiful body and earns a portion of her livelihood with considerable anatomical exposure? Would any Orthodox Jewish man deny that she deserves tremendous respect for her mind, her body, and her commitment to Judaism?

---

4   Aron Heller, [Schoolgirl On Front Line] the Associated Press, December 28, 2011.

Could this same Orthodox Jewish man not have the same respect for his wife or significant other if she decided to pursue such interests? Should she be excluded from consideration as a woman of valor? No, no, and absolutely no are the obvious answers.

With these questions being asked and answered, how is change to be effected? Where do we go from here to make something happen?

CHAPTER 4…SELF ESTEEM 101: DR. MARTIN LUTHER KING JR.

"Our Orthodox Jewish sisters have not yet recovered their collective self-esteem. However, when this does occur (and it will) their collective power will be unstoppable, much like a calving glacier, and the roar of its thunder will be unmistakable."

— Charles R. Krivcher, 2012

Orthodox Jewish women (not just in Israel) allow themselves to be robbed of their self-esteem, their natural rights, and their equal access to God simply because of their gender. The result is very disturbing to me. What should be taking place in Israel and around the world is a nonviolent movement to demand equal protection under the law, God's law. It should be a struggle akin to America's civil rights movement, as led by the late Dr. Martin Luther King Jr.

Interestingly, in one of Dr. King's finest speeches, "Where Do We Go From Here?"[5] he addressed many of the same issues that African Americans faced as they sought equal protection under the law. Dr. King's words, and the crux of the movement generally, are worthy of study by every Orthodox Jew. Allow me to quote from his speech and to insert in italics my substituted phrases. After reading the excerpts below, I recommend that you turn to appendix 3 and review the full text of Dr. King's original speech. Then draw your own conclusions.

> The tendency to ...strip *Orthodox Jewish women* of their personhood, is as old as the earliest history books and as contemporary as the morning's newspaper. To upset this cultural homicide, the *Orthodox Jewish woman* must rise up with an affirmation of *her* own *womanhood*. Any movement for the *Orthodox Jewish woman's* freedom that overlooks this necessity is only waiting to be buried. As long as the mind is enslaved, the body can never be free. Psychological freedom, a firm sense of self-esteem, is the most powerful weapon. ... The *Orthodox woman* will only be free when *she* reaches down to the inner depths of *her* own

---

5   August 16, 1967, the Southern Christian Leadership Conference [Atlanta, Georgia].

being and signs with the pen and ink of assertive *womanhood her* own Emancipation Proclamation. And, with a spirit straining toward true self-esteem, the *Orthodox Jewish woman* must boldly throw off the manacles of self-abnegation and say to *herself* and to the world, "I am somebody, I am a person. I am a *woman* with dignity and honor.

It is my feeling that Dr. King would be honored to have his strategies applied by today's Orthodox Jewish women. He might tell them that change is possible despite setbacks and remind them that in 1831, US Attorney General Roger Brooke Taney (who later became chief justice of the US Supreme Court and who wrote the majority opinion in the 1857 case of *Dred Scott v. Sandford*) "issued an opinion that upheld the power of southern states to prohibit free blacks (from other states or the British Empire) from entering their borders."[6] Professor Irons continued, in Mr. Taney's words, "The African race in the United States even when free, are everywhere a degraded class, and exercise no political influence. The privileges they are allowed to enjoy, are accorded to them as a matter of kindness and benevolence rather than right."[7]

---

6   Peter Irons, *A People's History of the Supreme Court* ([New York, New York]: Penguin-Putnam, 1999), 143.

7   Ibid.

Dr. King might observe that when Orthodox Jewish women are not allowed to be counted as persons in the formation of a minyan or to serve as cantors or rabbis or to sit front and center, they are quite without power. Dr. King would likely encourage them in the strongest possible terms to learn from history and simply rise up to demand equality from their Orthodox rabbis and synagogue presidents. If necessary, he would implore them to seek attention in the media. Quite frankly, it may take all of this and more to achieve real equality.

Dr. King continued (with my italicized modifications),

Another basic challenge is to discover how to organize our strength in terms of economic and political power. No one can deny that the *Orthodox Jewish woman* is in dire need of this kind of legitimate power. Indeed, one of the great problems that the *Orthodox Jewish woman* confronts is *her* lack of power. ...The *Orthodox Jewish woman* has been confined to a life of voicelessness and powerlessness. Stripped of the right to make decisions concerning *her* life and destiny, *she* has been subject to the authoritarian and sometimes whimsical decisions of this *male Orthodox Jewish* power structure. *Her place in the back or off to the side during religious services is evidence of an invisible wall that always serves to characterize her as a nonentity. This wall, this* ghetto, was created by those who had power (*Orthodox male leadership),* both to confine those who had no power and to perpetuate their powerlessness. The problem of transforming the ghetto, therefore, is a problem of power-confrontation of the forces of power demanding change and the forces dedicated to the preserving of the status quo. Now power properly understood is nothing but the ability to achieve purpose. It is the strength required to bring about...change.

Unfortunately, our Orthodox Jewish sisters have not yet recovered their collective self-esteem. However, when this does occur (and it will), their collective power will be unstoppable, much like a calving glacier, and the roar of its thunder will be unmistakable. As an aside, if you have never visited the Hubbard Glacier on Alaska's southeastern coast, it is a trip for everyone's bucket list. Its spiritual magnificence is overwhelming to say the least. Ma Generale and I have made two trips there via cruise ship, the first in 2006 aboard Holland America's *Westerdam* and again in 2010 aboard Holland's *Rotterdam.* For anyone in search of God's majesty and a universal feeling of spiritual awe, a visit to the base of the glacier to hear the thunderous roar of the calving ice is the end of the line.

The sea approach takes you from the Gulf of Alaska into Yakutat Bay and finally, into Disenchantment Bay. This voyage, which has been experienced by sea travelers for over 120 years, must have been as awe inspiring in 1888 as it is today. I have talked with many fellow cruisers in my time, many of whom have told me that they offered prayers to God during their visit to the glacier. Indeed, I have walked the ship's promenade deck during such visits and witnessed the cultural, religious, and ethnic diversity of the passengers, as nearly everyone called on his or her faith or spirituality in an effort to fully absorb the beauty of this natural wonder. We were all there together, all simple, mortal beings confronted with the majesty of God's work: Christians, Jews, Muslims, Hindus, Buddhists, Sikhs, and hosts of others; Americans, Canadians, Mexicans, Philippines, Japanese, Chinese, Russians, Israelis, Egyptians, British, French, South Africans, Australians, people from every country around the globe; all of us equal, all just people, all with prayers traveling to the same God, giving thanks for the same experience. And I am quite certain that the prayers from each person were not filtered or triaged by God based on country, religion, race, or gender.

However, I ask you to consider the following scenario: If ten of the passengers, who happen to be Orthodox Jewish women, wish to organize a minyan and to that end solicit the services of an Orthodox rabbi (who happens to be nearby on deck) for leadership, what is the rabbi to say? Under the current state of Orthodoxy's protocols, his answer would have to be something on the order of "No, let's wait until our afternoon prayers, when all the members of your respective families can participate" or "This is not the best time. It's very cold out here on deck, so we should move inside, where perhaps we'll find your other family members" or "My prayer book is in my cabin. Please give me about ten minutes to retrieve it. In the meantime, see if your family members would like to join us back here on deck." I have no doubt that the rabbi would be gentle, soft-spoken, kind, and accommodating in any way possible in order to allow the group to be enlarged by ten Jewish men.

But wait. What if the excuses run dry as the women press for an answer: "Rabbi, our husbands, sons, and daughters are playing bingo and do not wish to join us here on deck" or "Don't be silly, Rabbi, we don't need your prayer book. Let's just proceed impromptu and offer our prayers from the heart. We'll even take turns reciting prayers that are meaningful to all of us" or "Please help us now, as we are all swept up in the minute as the ship is turning to provide the best possible view of God's handiwork." Again, what is the rabbi to say?

He must say no, and I say he must think about why this has to be the case. Moreover, it is unlikely that he would or could look these women in the eye and proclaim with clarity that their souls are less important, inferior, subservient, and without equal value or merit as the souls of their husbands, sons, brothers, and other males. It is also unlikely that he will say that God will say no to the receipt of their prayers as a group or that ten female souls cannot or will not be characterized as a minyan. Why? Because it would be hurtful and demeaning to do so, and no Orthodox rabbi is going to deliver such a direct and verbal assault on the self-esteem of anyone. Besides, such a discussion is not likely to happen in public and out in the open, because the position to say no to these women is indefensible from a logical perspective and violates every notion of fair play that we practice day in and day out.

Further, can the rabbi be 100 percent certain that he is correct in his position? I say that in good conscience he cannot, and I ask him and every other Orthodox rabbi to simply find a way to say, "Yes, of course, let's form a minyan and pray." It is my feeling that saying yes would constitute a blessing of constitutional proportion and that God would be pleased. Alas, what are these men waiting for, and why are they afraid to say yes? Who would be harmed by such inclusion? One thing seems certain: drawing the rabbi out into an open discussion on the merits will likely be helpful in effecting change.

This being said, I am certain that Orthodox Jewish women will one day awake to discover that it is absolutely ridiculous to endorse, or to give any credence whatsoever, to the actions of any man or group of men working to assert power over them based solely on gender. Simply stated, the legitimacy of any such action or rule that marginalizes their equal value and equal access to God is fatally flawed. *Marginalize* is former Secretary Hillary Clinton's term, which I like very much. It seems to encompass the entire spectrum of schemes by which men have used their understanding of God to overreach women and to make them subservient. It is my hope that this awakening, this discovery that leads to the development of assertive power is close at hand.

Leadership from the pulpits of Orthodox Jewish rabbis will aid in this discovery process. I call on every American Orthodox Jewish rabbi to consider a two-step process. First, he must look squarely into the mirror, examine his conscience, and admit that equal access to God is a natural right, not to be infringed on by any person. Second, he should step onto his pulpit and into the boardroom of his synagogue, assume his role as spiritual leader, and speak clearly in support of bringing down the apartheid-like walls of inequality for women. I can almost sense the words of former President Ronald Reagan when on June 12, 1987, he declared in a speech at the Brandenburg Gate near the Berlin Wall, "Mr. Gorbachev, tear down this wall. ...The wall cannot withstand freedom."

Some additional thoughts for the Orthodox rabbis involve how we as Jews see ourselves as well as how we treat each other, all of which I will summarize from my perspective as a lawyer, retired soldier, and Reform Jew. To begin with, as a natural and unalienable right, every human being possesses the same standing to communicate with God, something I like to call equality in prayer and religious practice. Arguably, it is a natural right in the very same way that life, liberty, and the pursuit of happiness were asserted to be by Thomas Jefferson, John Adams, and fifty-four others in the Declaration of Independence.

As an aside, please recall that in 1776 King George III was certain that he was right and was therefore not amenable to substantive change. Such a natural right may not be legitimately infringed on by any power, and it has become my personal litmus test for any religious protocol to ask if in fact *equal* means equal. It seems to me that not unlike the protections afforded in America's Constitution and Bill of Rights, women are entitled to equal protection under God's law. It is fair to say that male-dominated Orthodox Judaism globally continues to infringe on the natural rights of Orthodox Jewish women. And, notwithstanding the courageous work done by so many brave women and women's organizations, so much more must be done. The time for action is now! People must be able to realize their full potential, regardless of gender.

Third, my instincts tell me that within the Bible, at least in the Old Testament, God had one overriding goal for a developing relationship with the children of Israel. God needed to ensure that these Jews did not revert to their old habit of worshiping idols or to otherwise turn away from the path of righteousness. As such, many of the procedural instructions, rules, and religious regulations proscribed (especially in the Torah) were meant to create a sort of divinely inspired firewall between Jews (trying desperately to reach Israel) and the pagan populations surrounding them. Is such a firewall necessary today? I think not and have no reservations in reaching this conclusion!

God, as the ultimate risk manager, completely understood and identified human strengths, weaknesses, and vulnerabilities and in later years used the prophets to offer carrots on sticks (my terminology) to continually seek their return to straight paths. Somewhere along the timeline of history,

Orthodox Judaism lost sight of the fact that times change, and as a result, these rules and so on (as part of the firewall) need to change as well. Further, I am aware of no written orders from God declaring that women should be excluded from assuming leadership roles within this process. Orthodox rabbis will simply have to look in the mirror, step forward, and lead.

Those of us with military experience know that you can't lead from behind. That being said, I am also unaware of any written orders from God that declare that a woman cannot become a cantor or rabbi or lead from the front of the congregation, from the pulpit. How patronizing and outrageous is this Orthodox limitation! How arrogant and self-serving it is coming from the pen and paper of men (not from God). Where would Orthodox Jewish men obtain such arbitrary power, to be exercised with such assuredness and unquestioned authority?

Surely God's guiding principles (the Ten Commandments, for example) remain as valid today as they were thousands of years ago and serve as a constitution of sorts for everyone. Beyond constitutional principles, the procedural rules and regulations for worship, developed by Jewish men, simply become part of our tradition. We all know that traditions change, with newer ones forming in place of older ones when appropriate. Thus, any tradition becomes a work in progress and should not be regarded as a strict principle, but rather as a tool to enhance the worship experience for everyone. *Everyone* is the operative word. After all, as was said by Malachi, "Hath not one God created us?" (Malachi 2:10). Thus my questions remain: are we not all equal in the eyes of God? Are the souls of men and women not the same?

As a practical matter, I am not certain where Orthodoxy became male dominated, and quite frankly that is not the concern of this work. This book is about the courage to change and the willingness to share power in such a way as to acknowledge that every human being (regardless of gender) begins on a level playing field, each in possession of a soul and moral compass, and the free will to follow it along God's path. Unfortunately, this oversight by Orthodoxy has relegated women to a position of beloved yet patronizing subservience, while men (responsible for updating the rules) have moved forward, making and remaking the rules at their pleasure.

All this being said, Dr. King might ask, "Where do we go from here"?

CHAPTER 5...OUR PERSPECTIVE CHANGES OVER TIME

"Yes, but the answers are all different."

– Dr. Thomas Childers

———••———

Because the Torah and its directives were written thousands of years ago, I am reminded of a story, told by Dr. Thomas Childers, professor of history at the University of Pennsylvania. At the beginning of his lecture series "A History of Hitler's Empire,"[8] he tells the story of a father who attends his daughter's college graduation and encounters his old history professor. In his conversation with his old teacher, the father points out that he could not help but notice that his daughter's exam questions were exactly the same as they had been when he was a student. The professor smiles and says softly, "Yes, but the answers are

---

8   *The Third Reich, Hitler and the 20th Century*, 2nd ed., disk one, the Teaching Company Limited Partnership, 2001, www.teach12.com.

all different." In his lecture, Dr. Childers goes on to explain that while facts do not change, we do, as does our interpretation of those facts.

Thus, it is an understatement to propose that the position occupied by women today is clearly different from that of several thousand years ago. As such, should the rules be the same? The rhetorical answer is "of course not." As an example, we do not stone people as prescribed in the Torah, sacrifice animals, or shave women's heads. Therefore, if changing certain rules is okay, why are Orthodox Jewish rabbis seemingly unable or unwilling to free Orthodox Jewish women from antiquated practices? After all, Jewish feminists are not trying to threaten or destroy Orthodox Jewish men, only to level the playing field.

Dr. Childers is fond of saying that in our respective processes of historical analysis (when we study history), it is helpful for the student to "forget what you know," to which I add the moral imperative "do what is right." My hope is that Orthodox rabbis can take the lead regarding this issue, forget what they know, and proceed with courage to make changes, to make blessings.

CHAPTER 6...BRINGING ORTHODOX RABBIS ON BOARD

"I distrust those people who know so well what God wants them to do, because I notice it always coincides with their own desires."

– Susan B. Anthony

"**S**oooooooo," as my wise sister, Harriet likes to say, what will it take to get Orthodox rabbis on board, to secure their buy-in, and to begin opening doors for women? My proposal asks Orthodox rabbis to think and act as individuals with regard to the compelling issue of women's equality. I ask that each of them envision a modern-day administrative hearing of sorts with God presiding, listening to all the arguments. With the underlying assumption that God is fully attuned to our civilization's march of progress, I ask that each Orthodox rabbi try to imagine the substance of God's ruling with regard to women. In a nutshell, I am asking each rabbi to get slightly outside the box, outside his comfort zone, and to seize the initiative, to anticipate the fact that God would bring the Torah up to date in a way that recognizes human progress in the twenty-first century.

This being said, the imagined hearing will have to be divine in nature, inasmuch as all Orthodox rabbis are certainly aware that in the United States there is no judicial review for matters involving ecclesiastical laws and faith. Thus, because the US Constitution and its interpretation by the US Supreme Court precludes such judicial oversight as a means of protecting religious freedom and the exercise thereof, the practical result is that if the rabbi says it is so, then it is so. Who is to question such authority, and what happens if one disagrees with rabbinic conclusions?

On this subject, I can recommend an article written by Professor Daniel R. Gordon of St. Thomas University School of Law.[9] Professor Gordon retired in May 2011. Among other cases, Professor Gordon analyzes the relatively recent case of *Klouda v. Southwestern Baptist Theological Seminary*, and its reliance on the US Supreme

---

9   [Gender, Race and Limiting the Constitutional Privilege of Religion as a Haven for Bias; The Bridge Back to the Twentieth Century], *Women's Rights Law Reporter* 31, no 4: 369-84.

Court's ruling in *Watson v. Jones*.[10] Professor Gordon writes,

In 2008, a United States District Court found that a school of theology could terminate the employment of a female assistant professor because she was a female. The District Court rejected the professor's claim that she possessed the right to be free of gender discrimination. The right to be free of gender discrimination acceded to the right of religious institutions to discriminate under the First Amendment of the United States Constitution. The District Court decision implicates the role of American religion as a constitutionally protected haven for bias and bigotry. This article examines how religious organizations and theology serve as repositories of discrimination.[11]

Dr. Gordon continues,

The *Klouda* Court relied on *Watson v. Jones* to explore the ecclesiastical abstention doctrine. The *Watson* Court found that civil courts should avoid taking jurisdiction over ecclesiastical subject matter to prevent depriving

---

10   Cited as 543 F. Supp. 2d 594 (N.D. Tex. 2008); and 80 U.S. 679 (1871).

11   [Gender, Race and Limiting the Constitutional Privllege of Religion as a Haven for Bias; The Bridge Back to the Twentieth Century], 369.

ecclesiastical bodies of construing their own church laws. The civil courts should avoid exercising jurisdiction over matters concerning theological controversy, church discipline, ecclesiastical government, or the conformity of the church to the standard of morals required of them.[12]

Professor Gordon also points out the often-ignored and practical result of settled American jurisprudence in this area of the law. "American religion remains immune from the legal pressures to treat all Americans equally and to avoid discrimination."[13] With these rulings in mind, I again reiterate that when the rabbi says it is so, it is so.

Therefore, with a clearer understanding of the rabbi's power and responsibility for leadership, let's return to my efforts to win over the individual judgment of the Orthodox rabbi. Let us return to the administrative hearing as God takes the microphone. Called to testify before God are three of America's most respected rabbis and three cantors. The Reform and Conservative clergy (four of the six) happen to be women, and the Orthodox clergy are both men. After their respective arguments, God thanks the rabbis and cantors

---

12   Ibid., 372.

13   Ibid., 376.

for their testimony and removes a reference book from a nearby book case. God begins to formulate an opinion for the group: "The world has come a very long way in a few thousand years. It is important for you to understand that in order 'to meet contemporary exigencies, modifications have to be introduced in traditional Jewish thought and practices.'" God continues, "Judaism must be 're-sponsive to the changing religious, moral, social, and economic needs of the Jewish people. "Judaism, in its periods of vitality, far from being a static, self-contained datum, was the developing religious culture of a people that could assimilate influences from other cultures and yet retain its distinctive ethos."[14]

God puts down the book and continues, "The very presence of these female rabbis and cantors should be clear and convincing proof to everyone that when any woman chooses to follow her dream and her heart into a life of rabbinic service or into service as a cantor, she must be accepted or reject-ed based solely on her merits and without consid-eration of gender. If accepted, she must be wel-comed wholeheartedly and without reservation or limitation of any kind. It is not necessary to spell out every detail of appropriate behavior for men

---

14 *The Standard Jewish Encyclopedia*, [Conservative Juda-ism], p. 479.

and women centuries following my delivery of the Torah, but rather, it is My guidance, My concept of fair-mindedness that human beings are capable of taking the initiative to adopt new traditions as they see fit as long as they are consistent with the spirit of Torah." The hearing is concluded.

This imaginary set of circumstances underscores both the power and responsibility possessed by Orthodox rabbis. If Orthodoxy remains committed to excluding women from the clergy and so on, there is no judicial review and thus no recourse for women, with two exceptions. The first involves willful religious disobedience, where women just say "no more," where they refuse to yield. The second is for women to simply walk away, to leave Orthodoxy and flee into the open arms of Reform and Conservative congregations where they are welcomed and treated as equals in every regard. I would take no pleasure in this second course of action; my only point is that Orthodox rabbis must understand the possible ramifications of failing to make needed changes. I appeal to their experience, analytical skills, and willingness to see all sides of this question. I am looking for rabbis with the "wisdom of Solomon," leaders who will make the hard decision to effect change because it is the right thing to do. Surely, freeing women in a way that brings them to equal status with men, and therefore, equal access to God should feel liberating indeed.

Even the US Marine Corps no longer advertises that it is "looking for a few good men" for the simple reason that women have proven themselves to be able Marines (again, that's a separate subject for another day). Orthodoxy can certainly find a way to do the right thing for so many millions of women in its ranks by allowing them to become able rabbis and cantors.

CHAPTER 7...CONCLUSION

"Just as Rosa Parks refused to move to the back of the city bus in Montgomery, Alabama, on December 1, 1955, so must American Orthodox Jewish women begin their refusal to be pushed down. Their continued submission simply empowers those who would overreach them."

– Charles R. Krivcher, 2012

———•———

The questions for Orthodox Judaism's male leadership are simple. First, would men be pleased if the tables were turned and they found themselves figuratively standing in the shoes of women, unable to serve as rabbis or cantors, pressured by women to dress in ultraconservative clothing, confined to worship in the back of the sanctuary or behind a curtain, and deemed invisible for the purpose of forming minyan? And second, would such treatment be fair? As before, the obvious answers are no and no.

Suggesting that we turn the tables is not a new concept. In 1896, the famous civil rights lawyer

Albion Tourgee represented Homer A. Plessy before the US Supreme Court.[15] In this famous civil rights case, the court disappointedly voted to uphold the Jim Crow law. My focus is not on the opinion itself, but rather on Tourgee's legal brief and his oral argument to the sitting justices. Professor Peter Irons describes the situation, which I now implore every ordained Orthodox rabbi to consider and then take to heart:

> Tourgee's brief to the Supreme Court reflected his refusal to temporize; he threw caution to the wind and challenged the justices to look racism in the face. "Suppose a member of this court, nay, suppose every member of it, should wake tomorrow with black skin...and traveling through that portion of the country where the 'Jim Crow car' abounds, should be ordered into it by the conductor. It is easy to imagine what would be the result, the indignation, the protests, the assertion of pure Caucasian ancestry. But the conductor, the autocrat of Caste, armed with the power of the State conferred by this statute, will listen neither to denial nor protest."
>
> Tourgee continued his philippic: "What humiliation, what rage would then fill the judicial mind! How would the resources of language

15   *Plessy v. Ferguson,* 163 U.S. 537 (1896).

not be taxed in objurgation! Why would this sentiment prevail in your minds? Simply because you would then feel and know that such assortment of citizens on the line of race was a discrimination intended to humiliate and degrade the former subject and dependent class,—an attempt to perpetuate the caste distinctions on which slavery rested."[16]

With this historical example in mind, I would like for every Orthodox rabbi to spend just a few hours behind the curtain during services or to stand within the ranks of a group of Jewish women trying to comfort one another in prayer—that is, desiring to form a minyan. I want the rabbi to look directly into their eyes as he lets them know in no uncertain terms that they cannot be counted and that God does not wish to hear their prayers as a group. I want him to feel the proximity of their humiliation, to fully understand what it means to be deemed invisible, how it feels to be in the second-class line, waiting to pray as a group.

If the rationalized response by Orthodox Jewish men is that there is no inequality, but rather a difference in roles, as long as women have a choice in their role and the rules are construed to be mutually applicable, some common ground might exist. For example, the minyan issue would be

---

16   Irons, *A People's History,* 226.

immediately solved if everyone is to be counted. The path to becoming an Orthodox Jewish rabbi or cantor would no longer be limited to men. With regard to where everyone would sit in synagogue (if indeed, it is necessary for men and women to be separated), a mutually applicable solution might envision a schedule whereby women would occupy the front and center seats in even-numbered years, with men occupying those seats in odd-numbered years, or vice versa. To do otherwise does not appeal to our sense of fair play, a concept we teach our children at an early age. To suggest otherwise reminds me of an expression used by a former circuit court judge in Memphis. Judge Irving M. Strauch was fond of saying on the record (and for emphasis), "It just ain't fair."[17] Ironically, Judge Strauch was Jewish.

This is a good time for me to reiterate that in no way whatsoever do I wish to direct the development of any human being's personal relationship with God (procedurally or substantively). My purpose is simply to preempt any person or group from overreaching another, and the litmus test is easy: if *equal* means equal, it's okay.

Again, the role of Orthodox rabbis is critically important and cannot be overstated. The need for them to lead by example becomes even more

---

17   [from personal observation of Judge Strauch on the bench]

compelling with regard to those women who do not see themselves as victims (that is, those who willingly accept their place at the back of the synagogue or at the back of the bus; those who respectfully and quietly acquiesce in their inability to be counted as equal persons to form a minyan or to become cantors or rabbis; or those who believe that they would be less Jewish or less holy if they simply let their hair down or dress as they please in public). For them, change may not be as important as simply having unrestricted freedom to choose both the role they wish to play and how they wish to play it. The individual woman's ability to make a choice without judgment or guilt from any man is the key. In any event, women will need compassionate reassurance from their rabbis in order to know that such monumental paradigm shifts are okay. They will need to know that they are no less Jewish or worthy of God's blessing simply because they choose a more modern approach to finding God in the twenty-first century (5774).

Victory will not be easy, and the stakes are high. Our Orthodox brothers continue to posture themselves in a soft-spoken yet powerfully controlling manner, now systemic to the infrastructure of Orthodox Judaism. In my judgment, any Orthodox Jewish rabbi who does not seize the pulpit and declare the wrongness of such discrimination will bear part of the blame if Orthodox Jewish men are ultimately found to be mean spirited or condescending (something no one wants). That being said, I wonder how these men will react when women as a group begin to say no in a clear and convincing voice, when they refuse to vacate the front row of the synagogue or refuse to wear certain clothing. If rabbis refuse to act, a sort of civil disobedience in the synagogue might very well become the order of the day, with all manner of social and news media in attendance. Or, as I mentioned earlier, women may simply choose to walk away.

In America, the place my grandfather called "the promise land," equal protection was brought to fruition by the civil rights movement, which taught us the meaning of words like *respect* and *equality*. Just as Rosa Parks refused to move to the back of the city bus in Montgomery, Alabama, on December 1, 1955, so must American Orthodox Jewish women begin their refusal to be pushed down. Their continued submission simply empowers those who would overreach them and is not unlike the plight of abused women whose continued submission empowers the abuser.

As relates to its women, Orthodox Judaism would do well to embrace the moral imperative offered by Dr. Childers, who admonishes us to "be vigilant about your rights; to care about the fundamental rights and human dignity of others. When the rights of any group, no matter how marginal or how small are violated, your liberty, your freedom is put at risk." For me, it is not only a bitter disappointment but terribly ironic that the only people on the planet who seem intent on treating Orthodox Jewish women as second-class persons are Orthodox Jewish men. The world must look on in wonder. Yet such observation pales in comparison to the possibility that God looks on as well, questioning why these otherwise kind and spiritual Jewish men seem incapable of exercising their free will to effectuate positive, egalitarian change, designed with one purpose only: to set women free.

In the first introductory paragraph of this work, I mentioned that making such changes will require immense courage on the part of Orthodox rabbis who will have to take the lead in this effort. It is completely coincidental and without planning of any sort that my congregation's two rabbis, Senior Rabbi Mark Schiftan and Rabbi Shana Goldstein-Mackler, delivered High Holy Days' sermons that more than touched on the subject matter of this book. Rabbi Schiftan spoke eloquently of our ability to make positive changes. Rabbi Mackler delivered clear and convincing thoughts about how to turn regret into the catalyst for change. At my request, they have allowed me to memorialize these two sermons by attaching them as appendices to this book. In my judgment, the persuasive power of their words, universal to all human beings, will forever stand the test of time. Their sermons are especially worthy of review, because as Orthodox Jewish women struggle for equality, their search for leadership will be ongoing. I place Rabbi Schiftan and Rabbi Mackler squarely at center stage, standing among an eclectic group of individuals whom I identify as being allies in support of equality for Orthodox Jewish women.

The famous trial lawyer and Jewish feminist Gloria Allred once observed, "Women should get a medal just for surviving. With each passing year, I become a more committed feminist. ...So my advice is that each one of us has a duty to help improve the status of women. The one thing I know is that we cannot let these wrongs go unaddressed. We need to make it a better world for our daughters, so they don't have to suffer the way we have suffered."[18] It is my hope that the distinguished Ms. Allred would endorse the proposals for change contained in this book.

Finally, it is my observation that even in the face of very persuasive assertions, Orthodox Jewish men will not release their grip on generations of self-serving religious preference, unless they

18   Bonnie Miller Rubin, *Fifty on Fifty*, Warner Books, Inc., New York, NY, 1998, [page3].

are pressured to do so by all of us as Jews. The obvious weakness in any argument that denies unequivocal equality for Orthodox Jewish women lies in the fact that such denial is completely illogical in the twenty-first century. Intended or unintended, the wall that protects Orthodoxy's systemic sexual apartheid will ultimately collapse under the weight of internal Jewish pressure, just as the Berlin Wall collapsed from its own internal pressures in 1989.

When the first American Orthodox synagogue (perhaps in Tennessee, Colorado, or Michigan) announces the called for changes, the dye will be cast for the rest to follow. A groundswell of support will grow into a contagion, and Orthodox Jewish women in Haifa, Boston, and Miami will ask their rabbis why they are not be able to sit front and center in services, serve their congregation as ordained rabbis or cantors, and be counted in the formation of a minyan. Again, are we not all God's children? Is not every soul worthy to appear before God on an equal basis?

One thing is certain. This emotional writing journey began with my father's simple instructions. It ends with my promise to deliver the same advice to my grandson. As this young man grows into maturity, it is my hope that he will have a smile on his face whenever he learns that a female Orthodox rabbi, standing at the head of her congregation, has welcomed her female congregants to services by saying, "Good morning, ladies. Welcome to the front row!"

POSTSCRIPT

———•———

Since completing *Welcome to the Front Row,* I took more than a few minutes to revisit a pair of reference books that occupy a special place on the shelves of my family's reading room, which I've read, reread, or listened to in audio format many times in recent years. They are *The Civil War: An Illustrated History* by Geoffrey C. Ward with Ric Burns and Ken Burns (Knopf, 1990) and *The War: An Intimate History, 1941–1945* also by Geoffrey C. Ward, based on a Ken Burns film with an introduction by Ken Burns (Knopf, 2007).

The introductory paragraphs of each were my inspiration for this postscript. First, from *The Civil War...*

> The Civil War was fought in 10,000 places, from Valverde, New Mexico, and Tullahoma, Tennessee, to St. Albans, Vermont, and Fernandina on the Florida coast. More than 3 million

Americans fought in it, and over 600,000 men died in it.[19]

In *The War* is the opening paragraph, which reads as follows:

The greatest cataclysm in history grew out of ancient and ordinary human emotions—anger and arrogance and bigotry, victimhood and the lust for power. And it ended because other human qualities—courage and perseverance and selflessness, faith, leadership and the hunger for freedom combined with unimaginable brutality to change the course of human events. The Second World War brought out the best and the worst in a generation. (at page xiv)"

For me, a retired soldier, the words and their message almost leap from the pages of these titanic books. While there will be no shooting war between Orthodox Jewish women and their male counterparts, for those women who insist on having a choice about the role they wish to play in Orthodox Jewish life, for those who will demand at least a level playing field, for those who feel strongly that ten souls to form a minyan means ten women or ten men, for those who feel strongly that their daughters should not be denied an opportunity to become Orthodox cantors or rabbis solely because of their gender, and for those who

---

19   p. xix.

wish to sit front and center for religious services in clothing of their choice, there is going to be a psychological war or at least a long series of protracted battles. They will struggle against overwhelming odds and against centuries of systemic apartheid. Their battles will take place in more than ten thousand places and will require tremendous individual courage and perseverance and the hunger for freedom to prevail.

These courageous women, dedicated to the proposition that their God-given natural rights cannot be taken by mortal men acting beyond the scope of God's instructions, must be respected as equal participants. In many cases, they will be emotionally drained, patronized, and excluded by men and perhaps ridiculed and shunned by other women. The battle lines will be formed in every Orthodox home, at the formation of every minyan, and in Orthodox synagogues wherever and whenever the discussion of equal status may arise and, most noticeably, whenever women are urged to yield but refuse to do so. Many of them will be afraid, not physically but psychologically and in ways that are difficult to overcome. Some may wish to carry a copy of *Welcome to the Front Row* or *Fight Back and Win* by Gloria Allred with Deborah Caulfield Rybak (HarperCollins, 2006). Allred's conclusion is powerful:

To win change however, you must be committed to making a change. Nothing gets done without sacrifice, discipline, resources, struggle and courage. You must understand that fear is a weapon that bullies use to keep women and minorities paralyzed and 'kept in their place'. "You must overcome that fear.

Remember that the denial of civil rights is not a small thing. It is an extremely important issue because it is about human dignity, which is everyone's birthright. When that dignity is not respected and when individuals are treated differently, subordinated, or excluded on account of factors over which they have no control—such as their gender, race, age, sexual orientation, or national origin—they and society are irreparably harmed. Freedom, liberty and equality are fundamental values that every human being should have a right to enjoy.

To those who suffer the daily indignity of discrimination and are treated as second-class citizens or as sexual objects, I say, '*Enough!*' Don't tolerate it for a single day or even a single minute. You have the power to stop it. You have more power than you believe you have. All you need to do is exercise your power.[20]

---

20 pp. 267-68, 270.

I am an eternal optimist, and it is my hope that the worst of our human emotions will retreat and that the best of them will prevail in order to preclude the necessity of civil disobedience in every conceivable Orthodox Jewish setting. Certainly Orthodox Jewish men led by wise Orthodox rabbis will be able to acquiesce to a set of changed behaviors toward women, one that permits everyone to win and through which God has our human assurances that the self-esteem of men and women will be enhanced and revered by the other.

SECOND POSTSCRIPT

Yom Kippur Evening, Wednesday, September 26, 2012
Notes from my home, Nashville, Tennessee

———

It has taken nearly one year to pen this book, and it seems altogether appropriate that some of this work's final words should be written on Yom Kippur after a day of prayer and reflection. It is late evening, and the house is quiet. Posh, my Siamese cat, sits on the desk beside the computer, and we are writing together (so to speak).

It's been quite a day. As a member of the temple's board of trustees, I was given the honor of a pulpit seat for morning services, my chair being positioned three to five feet behind the podium used by both of the rabbis and the cantor. Much of the service was conducted by the female members of the spiritual team, Rabbi Mackler and Cantor Fishbein. Rabbi Mackler delivered the Yom

Kippur sermon. Both of them read from the Torah along with our senior rabbi, Mark Schiftan.

From my pulpit view, it was possible to observe the faces of some nine hundred temple members and guests, all of whom seemed very accepting of female spiritual leadership. Not surprisingly, my thoughts in this book were intertwined with prayerful consideration of my many shortcomings. However, I suspect that it was my physical proximity to Rabbi Mackler and Cantor Fishbein that made the service even more meaningful. These two women have become such an integral part of the congregation, so woven into the fabric of all that characterizes who we are as Reform Jews in Nashville, Tennessee. Indeed, their respective leadership roles, their enhanced self-esteem, and their sense of personal accomplishment are also mine vicariously.

I wished that my Orthodox friends had been present to share this Yom Kippur experience. I wished with all of my heart that every Orthodox Jewish rabbi in America could have heard Cantor Fishbein as she sang Marshall Portnoy's "Meditation" on this holiest of days. It was as if her soprano voice was lifted to the skies by angels as she filled the sanctuary with these familiar prayers, made so breathtakingly beautiful that not a single person moved or made a sound. Indeed, for many in the congregation, this was their first opportunity to hear Cantor Fishbein. And suffice it to say when she began to sing this wonderful piece, the congregation seemed to hold its collective breath. At the time, it was my distinct impression that if every Orthodox rabbi had been in attendance, each would have been asked by the congregation how he or Orthodoxy could logically deny her right to be a cantor simply because of gender. Again, as Judge Strauch would have said, "It just ain't fair."

Finally, as I am writing this second postscript, I recall the shared advice of Rabbi Mackler, Cantor Fishbein, and Nancy Richardson, all of whom reminded me that my observations in this book are those of an outsider, as indeed I am. Additionally, Cantor Fishbein suggested that I reexamine Proverbs 31:10-31 (the passage on the woman of valor). "Take a look" she said. "It may say something to you." Her suggestion, delivered with a smile, seemed almost cautionary, filled with challenge and intrigue. I began to read it, to search for my own conclusions. This is the original text:

> Who might find a valorous woman, whose worth far exceeds pearls?
>
> Her husband trusts her deeply and he lacks for no riches.
>
> Each day she merits her family only good and never evil.
>
> She seeks wool and flax and gladly works with her hands.

She would trade like a sea merchant in order to obtain goods for her family.

She awakens late in the night to provide food for her family and wages for her staff.

She surveys land and acquires it, and grows a vineyard from her labor.

She keeps herself strong, and her arms are powerful.

She ensures her business dealings are successful and keeps her light on at night.

Her hands work the spinner and keep a firm grip on the spindle.

Her arms are open to the poor and she is generous to the destitute.

She does not fear for her family in the cold, for they are clothed in wool.

She makes her own carpets and wears clothing of white and purple.

Her husband is known in the city, where he meets with the elders.

She makes cloths for the markets and sells belts to the merchants.

She exudes strength and dignity and radiates joyous optimism.

Her mouth drips of wisdom and her words are kindness.

She maintains the decorum of her house and knows not of sloth.

Her children strive to please her and her husband to praise her.

Many are the women who have demonstrated valor, but you surpass them all.

Charm can be false, and beauty a ruse, but a God-fearing woman is truly praiseworthy.

Give due credit to her works and celebrate her through her accomplishments.

While also looking at a few pieces of interpretative writing provided by Cantor Fishbein, I formed an independent conclusion, perhaps one that the wise young cantor had already formed in her mind, as we had discussed my work some months before. With the benefit of hindsight, it occurs to me that she knew exactly what my conclusion would be, yet she wanted me to make the finding independently, without her having to point it out. She knew that reaching my own conclusions would provide a better learning experience for me.

I am told that in many Orthodox homes, this section of Proverbs is read aloud by husband to wife each Shabbat for the purpose of his letting her know just how much she is appreciated; it is certainly a kind and honorable tradition in itself. However, when considered in the totality of all the traditions within Orthodoxy, I am left with a disconcerting question, a troubling inconsistency. How could any man deny such a valorous woman the right to serve as a rabbi or cantor should she choose to do so? Would such traits and skills not be useful in Orthodox leadership roles both in the community and in the synagogue? How could anyone deny this woman of valor a place in the formation of a minyan or keep her from the front row of the synagogue or demand that she dress in a certain way? How could it be that she is more than capable of holding her own in the workplace, in society, in the business world, and yet without sufficient merit in the eyes of Orthodoxy to serve as a rabbi or cantor, or even to be counted in the formation of a minyan?

It seems to me that being counted for purposes of forming a minyan is among the most basic of all Jewish rights, something akin to the right to vote or to stand shoulder to shoulder with a man at the Wall in Jerusalem. Once women are given the right to form a minyan, the collateral restrictions on them will have to fall, simply because they will have to be construed as being inconsistent with all that we know to be fair. If a woman can be counted the same as a man before God, then can she be denied the right to become a rabbi or cantor? Can she be marginalized in any way? I think not.

I equate the power to join a minyan with African Americans' struggle to join the Union army during the American Civil War and to become citizens. Perhaps Frederick Douglas said it best when he observed the following in 1863: "Once let the black man get upon his person the brass letters, 'U.S.', let him get an eagle on his buttons and a musket on his shoulder and bullets in his pocket, and there is no power on earth which can deny that he has earned the right to citizenship in the

United States."[21] Similarly, let the Orthodox Jewish woman be counted in the formation of a minyan, and there will be no power on earth that can deny that she has earned the right to stand shoulder to shoulder with any man before God. It is no wonder that the wall that precludes her ability to participate fully, to enjoy equal access to God, is guarded so closely by Orthodox men. I would like to think that I am wrong about this and that Orthodox men would be delighted to welcome them into full and equal participation, if led persuasively by forward-thinking Orthodox rabbis. If this should happen, I will be among the first to say that I was wrong and give credit to almighty God for answering my prayers and perhaps the prayers of millions of others.

What must an Orthodox rabbi think when he reads an issue of *Reform Judaism* magazine, a magazine (as a voice for the movement) in which women and men are absolutely equal? Its very existence seems to establish a presumption that Orthodoxy's proclamation that women cannot occupy leadership roles is incorrect at best and overreaching at worst. Does he believe that these Reform Jews have taken complete leave of their senses?

---

21   Ward, *Civil War*, 246.

While this outsider is left with more questions than answers, suffice it to say that given everything contained in this book, it is my fervent prayer that the changes of heart, mind, and spirit that Rabbi Mark Schiftan discussed in his 2012 Kol Nidre sermon, "The Courage to Change" (see appendix 2), can resonate deeply with all Orthodox Jewish men. I pray that such changes will take place in a manner that allows Orthodoxy's women to feel empowered to seize their day and to emerge as magnanimous, equal participants, free to embrace the spiritual roles of their choosing. Perhaps then, in addition to the Orthodox man honoring his wife or significant other by reading the verses from Proverbs, he will follow up his words of acclaim with the right deeds. These deeds will speak louder than words; they will truly honor her value as a person and demonstrate his genuine desire to ensure that she is offered a seat on the front row, in the clothing of her choosing. From such deeds she will know that she is finally free to be all that she can be, wished to be, or dreams to be, by her own choice.

She will not have to provide limiting answers to her daughter upon becoming a Bat Mitzvah. The young woman's goals and dreams should be able to develop just as every thirteen-year-old Bar Mitzvah is assured by his rabbi and his parents that he is now a man in the eyes of God, that he is limited only by his imagination. Again, the litmus test is simple: does *equal* mean equal for everyone? When such changes are genuinely made to Orthodoxy's psychological infrastructure, just imagine the assurances that will be given by her rabbi and her parents when a thirteen-year-old girl becomes a Bat Mitzvah. Perhaps they will say with no regrets, "The sky is the limit for you, sweetie." I will say, "It's a good feeling, isn't it?" borrowing a line from Anthony Hopkins in the film *Meet Joe Black*.

However, regret may not be altogether negative; it may in fact have more power than we normally appreciate. In Rabbi Mackler's sermon delivered this past Yom Kippur at Congregation Ohabai Sholom, she analyzes our management of life's regrets during the High Holy Days (see appendix 1). She looks at regret positively, recognizing that seizing opportunities for changed behavior becomes our charge. She admonishes us to feel regret (as opposed to focusing on guilt), to learn from our experiences, and to make positive commitments to change.

This is no different from Dr. King's admonishment for us to be dissatisfied with the discriminatory status quo and to look to the future (see the end of his "Where Do We Go from Here?" speech). Thus, I wish for Orthodox Jewish men and especially Orthodox Jewish rabbis to feel regret for Orthodoxy's traditional limitations of women simply because of their gender. Feeling such regret, it is my hope that rabbis will work to effect changes that will liberate Orthodox Jewish women, setting them free to become equal participants before God. God will be a witness and will surely smile on each rabbi's initiative. Similarly, as Dr. King might suggest, if Orthodox Jewish rabbis will be dissatisfied with such discriminatory treatment of women and resolve to make positive change, a great emancipation will take place.

Over and over again I come back to the question of what an Orthodox Rabbi feels when he thinks of such issues, when he has coffee with female Reform or Conservative rabbis and sees the input of so many women in leadership roles. We would all like to know, because if deep within his heart he feels that a more egalitarian approach to accessing God would address many issues of fundamental fairness, then why is he not taking steps to initiate change? I sincerely hope that his answer is about freedom, equality, dignity, and self-esteem, about regret and the courage to effectuate change, and not about any concern for loss of control. His answer must also contemplate something more than his need to simply follow traditional orders. God has written no such orders, especially in the last few thousand years. Besides, in 2013, Professor Childers might again smile and say, "Forget what you know" and "Yes, but the answers are all different."

THIRD POSTSCRIPT

Sunday, September 30, 2012
The Madison Hotel, Memphis

———•———

Driven by one of life's passages, this third post-script is simply a digression for the purpose of inserting one last story in this book. It is in the predawn hours as I sit quietly at the desk in my hotel room (actually, a small suite with my beautiful Ilsa asleep behind cozy French doors). Later in the morning, she will ask, "Why have you made this addition, which is not so clearly relevant to your desire for women to reach the front row?" The straight answer is, "Because I can." But more importantly, our attendance at my forty-fifth high school reunion (Christian Brothers High School, Memphis) last evening brought the story to mind and has some bearing on bringing women to the front row.

I guess it was seeing many of my classmates for the first time in forty-five years and listening to their stories that brought back memories of my own, and in particular, a few that surrounded my mother's illness and death. Please recall that in chapter 2, I mentioned her passing, yet there was more to the story that I would like to share in this final postscript. I share it both as a tribute to the Catholic community I knew as Christian Brothers High School and as a snapshot of my feelings about prayer at the age of sixteen.

My mother, who suffered from diabetes, was by all accounts, the kindest, most gentle woman on the planet. Sadly, in early November 1965 when she asked that I drive her to the doctor, I sensed danger. I also recall that she packed a small bag in anticipation of being sent to the hospital. She died on December 14. This event delivered a shocking reality to my world, especially with regard to my appreciation for prayer. During those terrible six weeks, our circle of friends and family provided assurances that my mother was in their prayers. Coming from a myriad of faiths, all their prayers were genuine, heartfelt, and desperate. At my high school, I was humbled when the Christian Brothers' Principal (Brother Stephen) took me aside to advise that my mother's recovery had become a priority in their prayers. Indeed, when I returned home and told my dad that the Brothers were keeping mother in their prayers, it felt as though, alas, alas, the Catholic cavalry would arrive in time to carry the day.

During this pensive time, my father, one of my sisters, and I went to the temple sanctuary on a few occasions outside scheduled services. Sitting quietly, we prayed and wept intermittently while, just two miles away, the very best doctors of the day searched for a miracle. God did not intervene, and my mother's death at age fifty-two seemed so untimely. I wondered why God had not crossed the divine-earthly threshold to rescue this woman of such valor. Looking back, I see that my life experience was limited, and I had yet to see the big picture, God's picture. Indeed, God had many pressing issues. The civil rights leaders were certainly deserving of help, as were our troops in Vietnam, now dying in large numbers.

My faith persisted, and I continued to say my prayers in hopes that the next time it became necessary to line up at the prayer window for a specific withdrawal, it would not be necessary for me to reintroduce myself to God. I would certainly need to grow up more in the coming years, yet another of my principles was in development. I could not simply summon God's assistance for desired results, yet I needed a personal relationship with God. And though life continued despite the irreplaceable loss of my mother, I would never forget the willingness of the Catholic clergy to open their hearts, minds, and souls for this Reform Jewish student.

As these last words are written, it is not only my prayer (but also the point of this book) that Orthodox Jewish men find a way to open their hearts, their souls, and their minds for positive change—Rabbi Schiftan's style of change. I am quite certain that in doing so, each of their own lives will become a blessing and that God will applaud them for taking the initiative to perform perhaps the most noble of all deeds: to set their fellow human beings free and to begin making things right for future generations of women.

FOURTH POSTSCRIPT

"May the words of my mouth and the meditations of my heart be acceptable before you, O God my Rock and my Redeemer. May the One who makes peace in the heavens make peace for all of us."
(From "Meditation" by Marshall Portnoy as sung by Cantor Tracy Fishbein)

Wednesday, November 7, 2012
The American Cemetery above Omaha
Beach, Normandy, France

It is late morning, and Ilsa and I are walking arm in arm among the graves of heroes in this sacred American military cemetery. Marking the graves are Christian crosses and Stars of David. From the center, they are aligned in perfect order for hundreds of yards in every direction. For this retired soldier (for anyone really), the tears immediately flow with my first step onto this ground. Together with my wife's comforting voice, I recall with clear recollection the voice of Cantor Fishbein singing Marshall Portnoy's "Meditation."

On this hallowed ground, I thank God not only for the ultimate sacrifice of these brave soldiers who gave their lives for our freedom, but also for my Reform tradition, which allows the beautiful voice of this wonderful woman to be an integral part of my religious life. From this experience of being surrounded by fallen soldiers, I am brought to the final point of my book. Asking every Orthodox man to join me on a short journey, let us go back to soldiering in a different time and revisit the days of the American Civil War. Indeed, the plight of black slaves equates convincingly to that of today's Orthodox Jewish women.

It is widely known that the Confederacy argued almost to the end of the war that slaves could not be soldiers. After all, under the original US Constitution, they were considered to be only three-fifths of a person. And the United States Supreme Court, via its embarrassing opinion in the Dred Scott case, held that slaves could not be citizens; they were essentially items of personal property.[22] As the South's situation became more and more desperate, additional voices sounded the need for a change of heart in order to make soldiers of slaves. This sounds a lot like Orthodoxy's declaration that

---

22   60 U.S. 393, 1857.

women cannot become rabbis or cantors, or be counted in the formation of a minyan.

Consider the comments of General Howell Cobb of Georgia as he responded to the suggestion that slaves should be trained as soldiers:

> I think that the proposition to make soldiers of the slaves is the most pernicious idea that has been suggested since the war began. You cannot make soldiers of slaves, or slaves of soldiers. The day you make a soldier of them is the beginning of the end of the revolution. And if slaves seem good soldiers, then our whole theory of slavery is wrong.[23]

Thus, my final point is that, because Cantor Fishbein, Rabbi Mackler, and legions more just like them have proven themselves to be able congregational leaders, the whole theory of Orthodoxy's continued exclusion is wrong. In my heart, I am cautiously optimistic that Orthodoxy can look into its collective mirror and summon the courage to move forward, to feel regret, to effect change. It seems serendipitous that the Yom Kippur sermons of Rabbi Mackler and Rabbi Schiftan (as appendices 1 and 2) surfaced during the final stages of my writing. Their advice about learning from our regrets of past behaviors and finding the courage to make positive changes is perpetually

---

23 Ward, *Civil War*, 253.

relevant for all of us, particularly for Orthodoxy's leadership as it struggles forward. Maybe, just maybe, this will be the year that Orthodox Jewish women are wholeheartedly welcomed to the front row as equal participants, that *equal* can really mean *equal* for millions of women. If this occurs, all Jews can stand together and exclaim in one voice, "It's a good feeling, isn't it?"

APPENDIX 1

Rabbi Shana Goldstein Mackler,
"Living With Regrets"
Sermon delivered to The Temple, Congregation
Ohabai Sholom, Nashville
Yom Kippur 5773 (September 26, 2012)

———

Have you ever had a driveway moment? You know, it's when you are listening to something on the radio in the car, something that is so compelling that you sit in your car, in the driveway, after you've reached your destination. And you continue to listen to the story on the radio until it is finished. Last February, I had a driveway moment. There was a story on NPR about Roger Boisjloy, a former NASA engineer who had died. Boisjoly was one of five engineers who tried in vain to stop the Challenger from taking off that fateful day in 1986. He knew what would happen. He was paid to know these things. He tried to tell the people in charge; he tried to cancel the launch. He was right, but no one would listen. After the shuttle exploded, Boisjoly's life fell apart. He could not sleep; he hardly ate. He had to go on disability pay, because he could not keep it together at work.

Finally, he spoke out about what had happened, and resolved to make a difference. His whole life changed. And when he died, he acknowledged the regret that he held these 25 years. It was still there. It was part of him. But he died at peace. Fueled by the regret that he could have done more, Boisjoly changed his career path and built a life around ethical engineering—teaching students to make ethical choices and stick to the data—and to speak out.[24]

The journey Roger Boisjoly took goes right to the heart of the Day of Atonement. We find ourselves poised somewhere between admitting our wrongs, facing our regrets, and learning not to be burdened by them.

I tend to understand the sentiment of the iconic French singer Edith Piaf croons that she has no regrets, not the good, not the bad, and many seem to agree with her. But not me. I lean more toward the words of a blogger of a different faith who recently posted, "I don't believe you can live a life free from regret. You'd either be Jesus or a jerk—and at least a jerk says I am sorry from time to time!" What this social critic was evaluating was that people who

---

24   [http://m.npr.org/story/146490064] February 6, 2012.

claim to never regret anything either never made a mistake, or just don't care that they did, didn't feel badly for the pain that was caused, longed for the loss incurred, or mourned the opportunities that passed by.

We all have regrets. If you spend a moment on the web, you'll find regret support groups, for those things that we regret that others do too, from surgical procedures, to dating the same guy. A few years ago, University of Washington Hillel created post regret, where people can anonymously state their regrets to try to clear their slate for the coming year, and you may have even read this week in the NYT about people expressing their wishes, concerns, and yes, even their regrets for this year that were posted and displayed on a screen behind the rabbi during Rosh HaShanah services in Miami Beach.[25]

Consider a politician with a gaff that seems to never disappear of an NFL replacement referee with a questionable call. ...With hindsight, we often regret little things like a second or third trip to the oneg table, a hairstyle, or not buying Apple stock in the nineties. We may regret professional choices, educational choices, relationship choices. Regrets for what we've said and haven't said. Regrets for failing to stand up for someone or for

---

25 *New York Times,* September 18, 2012.

getting involved in what was not our business in the first place. Regrets for making excuses rather than making amends. Regrets for a status update or tweet we wish we'd never posted. We may regret how we have acted toward those with us today, our families sitting next to us, or just a few seats away, our friends how we have abused their trust and their love. We may regret what we have done to friends or acquaintances whom we pained with a thoughtless word or insensitive story. We may ache with regret for hurt done to those with whom we can never reconcile. Some regrets stay with us long after the events that caused them. They have a half-life measured in decades.[26]

Because we live in a culture, in a country, in a faith where we get to make choices, we have more regrets. The more responsibility we have for our individual lives, the more opportunities we have for making mistakes. We often get things wrong— sometimes for good reasons and sometimes not. Regret allows us to see it clearly and recalibrate. The key to using regret in a valuable, positive way is to harness all the good that can come from recognizing where we failed and resolving to do better. Regret, like all emotions, has a function for survival. It is our brain's way of telling us to take another look at our choices, a signal that our actions may

26 Thanks to Rabbi James Gibson.

be leading to negative consequences. Regret can motivate action to learn from our mistakes and to become a smarter, better person in the future. As Kierkegaard put it, "Life can only be understood backwards, but it must be lived forwards."

Bronnie Ware, a palliative care nurse, recently surveyed her patients in their final days. As she sat with them for the last weeks of their lives, she gleaned from them what they would have done differently, what they might regret. You may not be surprised that their answers reflect those behaviors most of us would choose to adopt now, rather than wait until we cannot change them. They regretted working too much, not being true to themselves, not allowing themselves to be happier, not spending enough time with family and friends. But each of them, by expressing their regrets, found a way to reconcile before they passed. They either made amends, or forgave themselves.[27]

Amongst Jews, the concept of regret is often confused with the concept of guilt. But they are not the same thing. Guilt can create paralysis. Regret creates redefinition. Guilt can be stunting, and we beat ourselves up reliving a moment again and again. It makes us blame ourselves, not our action or inaction. But regret? Regret stretches

---

27 *The Top Five Regrets of the Dying: A Life Transformed by the Dearly Departing.*

us to be better, greater, longer, longing versions of ourselves. Regret is *necessary* if the past has any hope of not repeating itself, or of creating itself from its ashes—of morphing into something new.[28]

An insightful person once said, We need *guilt* to keep us in line; we need *regret* to keep us coming back to the starting line. Despite the mistakes we will inevitably make, we continue to grow and learn. When we feel regret about something, it is instructive. It's like the *Journal of Negative Results* that was created a decade ago. A Harvard University scientist created a worldwide collection of mistakes, scientific failures, and thousands of other scientists contributed. Why? Why would they want to publish their mistakes and failures? Because they understood the value of trial and error, of learning from mistakes, as stepping stones to answers, solutions, and positive outcomes.[29] Healthy regret is such a useful tool that it is said in the Talmud that anyone who does a (sinful) deed and regrets it, is immediately forgiven. According

---

28 "Guilt vs. Regret and Forgiving Yourself" by Gene Monterastelli, with work on PTSD.

29 *This Is Not the Life I Ordered* by Deborah Collins Stephens, Michealene Cristini Risley, Jackie Speier, and Jan Yanehiro, 58.

to the level of regret, so is the change in one's heart.[30]

Those steps are built into the holiday. In fact, our tradition says that teshuvah, repentance, existed before the world was even created. We are human beings, fallible, and we are going to make mistakes, and our regret prevents us from making the same mistakes again. Teshuva, repentance, is not about making our mistakes disappear. It is about making them whole. As Rabbi Larry Kushner says, it is about looking deep within and finding the holy spark, even in our hurtful words and acts and letting that spark arise and move us to live and act differently. Regret, Resolve, Repair. Those are the steps in order. Acknowledge the shortcoming and regret; resolve that you will do better. Say what you mean, and mean what you say, and then do the work to repair the situation. In this way, Yom Kippur becomes a day of joy and reconciliation. Forgiveness comes from choosing to take responsibility for the past, learning from the past, and being present in the current moment making new choices. It is looking at our acts and accepting the rebuke from within. Taking the sting of regret

---

30 Rabbi Hanina bar Papa and Miamonides on *acharenta*. Thanks to Rabbi Elyse Goldstein and Rabbi Robert Harris for pointing out these texts.

and transforming it into something good. An apology. A recompense. A promise to do better.[31]

Another beautiful aspect of this holiday is that not only do we acknowledge and celebrate our humanity by allowing for imperfection and mistakes, not only do we get the chance to make right those things we did wrong in the past, but we also acknowledge that we will regret things in the future too. Indeed, that is what we chanted in the Kol Nidre prayer: "All of these things—all the vows, oaths and obligations we *will* make—we *already* regret them." As Rabbi Elyse Goldstein suggests, we already regret what we haven't done yet? Now that's Jewish guilt for you: I can preorder my regrets!

These High Holidays enable us to live with our regrets, to incorporate them into our lives as motivation, gratitude for who we are now. That is not the same as not having regrets. It means we've learned, we've grown, and we continue to become.

We are called upon to face our own mortality on these holidays, but two years ago, almost to the day, Edward Rosenthal really came face to face with his. He was on a day hike in Joshua Tree National Park when he took a wrong turn and strayed for thirteen miles before stopping and waiting for

---

31   Thank you to Dr. David Barton for his guidance and conversations about regret, guilt, and the growth that can happen through Yom Kippur.

help. For six days, in one-hundred-degree heat, he survived without food or water. He laid low, and being a writer, decided to leave messages for his family. Not having any paper, but always with a pen, Edward wrote to his family on his hat, telling them what kind of funeral he wanted—replete with Persian food for shiva—who they could trust and how much he loved them. He expressed his regrets and wrote about a vacation they had planned and how his wife should still go, how meaningful his relationships were, and that if his wife or daughter should ever get down, just to think of him, of how much he loved them, and that there was always hope.[32] All this he wrote on a hat, which he and his family have framed and cherish, as a reminder. It wasn't too late for Edward. It isn't too late for us.

Our challenge is to balance recognizing our regrets with being overburdened by them. This happens most often when we cannot change the situation, rectify it. We risk our regrets leading to fruitless rumination and self-blame that keeps people from reengaging with life. Yom Kippur allows us to get out from the overburdening weight of regret for things for which we had no control; it allows us the tools for self-compassion and forgiveness. Most importantly, we can begin the difficult task of forgiving ourselves.

---

32 *Los Angeles Times,* October 1, 2010.

So, if we know that our human condition mandates we will have regrets, and Judaism tells us we need them to grow and learn, but not to be smothered by them, how do we live our lives with as few regrets as possible? It comes down to seizing opportunities. That is what plagues many of us today—not the sins that we committed and about which we are now filled with regret. What causes us great angst are the things we might have done, but which we let pass by, and the things we want to do in the future, but fear we won't.

Most often, we regret what we *haven't* done more than what we *have* done. We regret *not* taking chances more than regretting the chances we actually took. And Yom Kippur reminds us we are held accountable for both.

In an ancient Greek city, there was a statue devoted to the god Caerus, the god of opportunity. Caerus is represented as a young and beautiful god. He's standing on tiptoe because he is always running with wings in his feet to fly with the wind. He holds a razor, or else scales balanced on a sharp edge—attributes illustrating the fleeting instant in which occasions appear and disappear. And he has a lock of hair in the front of his head, being bald in the back, telling us: you must grab him by the hair as he approaches, for once he has passed, opportunity can never be brought back again.[33]

Olympic gold medalist Aly Reisman knows a little something about seizing opportunity. But it wasn't just her athleticism that won the hearts of Jews around the world. When Aly won the gold, she knew she had one opportunity to make a statement for Jews of every nation who collectively mourned the loss of the 1972 Olympic Israeli athletes. Forty years later, this past summer, when the world would rather forget the tragedy, Aly chose to remember. Aly Reisman had one moment on the world stage, and she took it. She knew if she did not seize that opportunity to pay tribute to those athletes, she'd regret it for the rest of her life. What she could not foresee was the ripple effect it had around the Jewish world.

An officer in the Israel Defense Forces sent a letter to Aly after her performance, and posted it on her Facebook page.

Dear Aly,

I want to tell you about how you became the hero of a gym full of Israeli soldiers. …
    You picked a song for your floor routine in the Olympics that every Jewish kid

---

33 Greekgodsandgoddesses.com

knows, whether their families came from the shtetls of Eastern Europe, the Asian steppes of Azerbaijan, the mountains of Morocco or the Kibbutzim of northern Israel. It's that song that drew almost everyone at the Israeli army base gym to the TV as soon as the report about you came on the news this morning. After showing your floor exercise to Hava Nagila, the announcer told about your gold medal with unmasked pride, and of your decision to dedicate it to the Israeli athletes who were killed in the Munich Olympics in 1972.

There were some tough people at that gym, Aly. Men and women, battalion commanders from Intelligence, captains from the navy, lieutenants from the Armored Corps and more. You probably understand that words like "bravery" and "heroism" carry a lot of weight coming from them, as does a standing ovation (even from the people doing ab exercises.) There was nothing apologetic about what you did. For so long we've had to apologize for who we are: for how we dress, for our beliefs, for the way we look. It seems like the International Olympic Committee wanted to keep that tradition. Quiet, Jews. Keep your tragedy on the sidelines. Don't disturb our party.

They didn't count on an eighteen-year-old girl in a leotard.

There wasn't one person at the gym who didn't know what it was like to give back to our people, not one who didn't know what happened to the good people who died in 1972, not one who didn't feel personally insulted by their complete neglect in the London Olympics, the forty-year anniversary of their deaths, and not one who didn't connect with your graceful tribute in their honor.

Thank you for standing up against an injustice that was done to our people. As I was walking back to my machine at the gym, I caught one of the officers give a long salute to your image on television. I think that says it all.[34]

We may never know how far the effects of our actions travel. What we do know is that if we don't take that opportunity to say what needs to be said, to repair what we have broken, all those regrets, all those should haves, would haves, could haves from last year will not go away. Listen to the words of Rabbi Harold Schulweis: The last word has not been spoken, the last sentence has not been

---

34 Dan Yagudin, officer, Israeli Defense Force.

written, the final verdict is not in. It is never too late to change my mind, my direction, to say no to the past and yes to the future, to offer remorse, to ask and give forgiveness. It is never too late to start over again, to feel again, to love again and to hope again.

May this be so. Amen.

APPENDIX 2

Rabbi Mark Schiftan, "The Courage to Change"
Sermon delivered to The Temple, Congregation
Ohabai Sholom, Nashville
Kol Nidre 5773 (September 25, 2012)

———•———

R emember those light bulb jokes?

There's the one I love about the Jewish mother: How many Jewish mothers does it take to screw in a light bulb? "It's okay," she says, "I'm fine. I'll just sit here in the dark." Oy.

Then there's my favorite one, the one I love the most: How many therapists does it take to change a light bulb? Just one. But the light bulb has to want to change.

Change is hard. It is painful. Often, excruciatingly so.

It is hard for all of us—whether as a nation, as a community, or as a congregation. Or even as a single soul. Sometimes even more so that way.

Not all change is welcome. Unexpected test results, a newly discovered lump, an unanticipated move...other changes that we least suspected and that are most feared.

And yet, even then, we know that those very tests, or the early discovery of that lump, may either prolong life or keep death at bay. And that can be a blessing in the end.

On the other hand, constructive change is often for the good and can often make us and our lives better. Positive change is important as we grow up, and it becomes even more important as we grow older.

As a nation, we know this is true.

Consider this: Six weeks from today, we will go to the polls on Election Day. Two men, both of decent moral character—one an African American, the other a Mormon American—are the candidates of their respective political parties for the presidency of the United States. One of them hopes to reside in the White House; the other already does.

Let me ask you this: Ten years ago, who would have believed it could happen? Would we? Would you? What's next? A Jewish vice president? Oh, wait, that already happened, too. Well, almost. Oy.

As a nation, we've championed women's rights. We've fought for civil rights. And we are establishing same-sex rights, slowly but surely, whether for military service or for a marriage ceremony.

Are we the better for these changes? Of course we are. Without a doubt.

Our Jewish community has had to evolve as well. And we are the better because of these changes too.

There's a *New Yorker* cartoon that depicts the ancient Israelites crossing the Red Sea. Moses, staff in hand, is leading his people through the parted waters on dry land. Six hundred thousand Jews, all of them actually in agreement, all moving in one direction at a single, signal moment in time. The raging waters stand to their left and to their right, held back by the divine hand of their God.

At the front of the line, in the first row of marchers on the road to freedom and the Promised Land, right behind Moses, their leader, the one who Jewish tradition describes as the greatest prophet of all time, we see two of these members of the tribe talking with one another, or more likely arguing with one another about Moses. Of course, the caption reads: "Well, I mean he's okay as a leader. I just wish he was a little bit more pro-Israel!"

Let's be honest. Even then, we were a challenging and cantankerous nation, a chutzpadik and complaining people.

Those discussions and debates continue to this day. Last year, our Jewish community felt the pangs of civil discord regarding the varying views we all hold —and profess—regarding the challenges faced and presented by the State of Israel. Our Jewish community tried to find the path towards a more civil discussion and dialogue on that which unites us and that which divides us, and to do so honestly, yet respectfully. In fact, I spoke about it one year ago on that Kol Nidre night. Remember that sermon? Oy. Half of you knew exactly what I was talking about and the other half of you had no idea—then—what I was talking about. Okay: Maybe more than half. Oy. Anyway, you do now.

So one year later, where are we as a community? I'll tell you where. We allowed cooler heads and calmer hearts to prevail. We drew a line in the sand as to what our community would tolerate and what it would not accept. The Federation established an editorial board for our Jewish newspaper, the *Observer*; our Jewish Community Relations Committee formed a series of community conversations, culminating in a statement of our shared communal beliefs and behaviors (they are on panels, right in front of the entrance to the sanctuary); our temple, along with other synagogue boards and the boards of other Jewish organizations, signed on to a Civility Statement, inspired, in part, by the Nashville Board of Rabbis, and others; and we found the way to let many voices with different and even opposing views speak in our various Jewish venues in town.

Are we the better for those changes? You bet we are.

Were they easy to accomplish? Like a root canal. Without Novocain.

But worth it? Without a doubt.

We made changes as a congregation too. Some were easy; others less so. But the evidence of their positive impact on our congregational life is irrefutable now: We are a larger congregation than we were just two years ago; we are a younger congregation than we were just two years ago—of the sixty-four new memberships since the last High Holy Days, almost half of them are Jews under the age of thirty-three; we are a more diverse congregation than we were, just a few years ago; we are reaching more Jews on the periphery, in more areas of emerging Jewish populations, in more innovative programmatic ways, than we were just a few years ago; and we are welcoming Jews-by-birth, and especially Jews-by-choice, in ways and in numbers unimaginable just a few years ago. Together, this past year, we celebrated the first same-sex wedding in our congregation's history— a ceremony uniting the lives of two newly minted Jews, under the wedding canopy, the chuppah of the Jewish people. These two beautiful souls, along with other newlyweds and newly welcomed Jews by choice, carried the Torah scrolls through our congregation—now their congregation too—just a few days ago, on Rosh Hashanah morning.

I share this with you not in an arrogant nor boastful manner, nor as an statement of collective self-aggrandizement; I deliver this message as a shared acknowledgement of our collaborative, well-deserved, and well-earned congregational pride.

Did these successes come as a direct result of the many changes that we made? Absolutely.

Are we a better congregation because of all those who have come to call this place home? Absolutely.

Are we a more embracing, engaging, inclusive, enveloping congregation now than we were before? Absolutely.

Without a doubt.

So we have changed, as a nation, as a Jewish community and as a congregation. And we are the better for it. Without a doubt.

But what about us? What about you? And me? And us? What single, positive change could you decide to make—on this sacred night, and on this Day of Atonement—that would both better your life and better our world?

Let us be clear: Not every change is welcomed or desired; some are foisted upon us in unanticipated ways, and we have to respond in unexpected ways as well. Not every change is a good one, and we are acquainted with the difficulties presented by those circumstances as well. For those changes, in those cases, there is no silver lining—only the healing power of time and the healing embrace of community.

But, in all other circumstances, what one thing comes to mind for you—something of substance, that is, not of veneer—that you would like to change within you, that would both better yourself and improve the world? Something that would require a change of heart, of mind, or of spirit?

An example of a change of heart might involve something like this: Is there someone you've been avoiding because you don't know what to say to them? They're facing illness or loss or failure, and so you're so afraid of saying the wrong thing that you've chosen—by default—to say nothing at all? We've all been there. I've been there, too. The good and the bad news, I suppose, is that we're not alone.

I remember two specific rabbinic conventions from years past. Harriet and I arrive at the airport, gather our luggage, and enter the courtesy van to the hotel. The van is filled with several other rabbis, all of whom Harriet has known for years through her work for a URJ summer camp out west. One of the rabbis has just endured a challenging divorce.

The van is silent. Finally, Harriet—the one non-rabbi—looks the newly divorced rabbi in the eyes and asks him, "How are you doing? I'm not sure what to say: Sometimes these things are for the better and sometimes for the worst. I just wanted to let you know I was thinking about you." Upon hearing this, all of the other rabbis—yup, me too—are either looking out the window to survey their potential escape routes or looking under the seats for a place to hide. Hours later, at the convention, the recently divorced rabbi comes up to Harriet and me. "I have to thank you," he says to her. "No one's even mentioned it to me here, and I've known some of these people for thirty years."

A year passes, another convention, another van full of rabbis. And Harriet. One of the rabbis lost his wife during the past year, to cancer Again, silence. Except for Harriet. Again, she is the only one to convey her sympathies, to inquire about his emotional state of being. Hours after the conversation, he also approaches her. Same expression of gratitude. Turns out he's dating again. He's happy to share that too.

Look around this sacred space; search your heart as well. Someone, somewhere, is waiting to hear from you—either for your call or for your visit. They may be recovering from illness or still in the hospital or now in the care of hospice. They may have been the recipient of a bitter diagnosis or an even more bitter divorce. They may have lost a loved one recently or have simply lost hope in ever finding love again. Will you—will we—find the courage to change our hearts, to open them and our mouths as well? Will we find the words and the voice with which to share them? You want to know what to say to them and what they want to hear from us? Just the truth—that we are frightened too. They just want to hear the truth—that we still care about them. For until we find the words to speak to them, our silence is all that speaks for us. And it speaks volumes. All that it requires is a change of heart.

Perhaps the courage to change one thing in the year ahead involves a change of mind. As Rabbi Jonathan Sacks writes, "Teshuva (Repentance) tells us that our past does not determine our future. We can change. We can act differently next time than last. If anything, our future determines our past."[35]

What he means, I believe, is this: When we have a positive change of mind, we do more than open up a new chapter of our future; we also liberate a portion of our past.

So maybe it's as simple as having the courage to finally come to the place where we can to say "I'm sorry" to someone longing to hear those words; to arrive at the destination where we can

---

35 From a sermon by R. Stuart Weinblatt, as reprinted in UJC's *The Orchard*, Fall 2012.

finally acknowledge the hurt we may have caused another for an offensive remark or an insensitive comment made recently—or long ago.

Perhaps it means apologizing. Or apologizing again.

Or perhaps it means finding the courage to open our minds and our hearts to accept an apology—finally—and to finally grant someone a long-awaited forgiveness. You can take that anger to the grave with you or you can pray that the other guy gets there first, ahead of you, or you can bury that grudge, perhaps here and now.

It's Yom Kippur. If not now, then when?

Finally, we can have the courage to have a change of spirit. We can work to improve the lives of others as well. We can expand our efforts at tikkun olam, in repairing the world, even as we better their worlds too.

As former Secretary of State Condoleezza Rice recently remarked, the essence of America—that which really unites us—is not ethnicity, or nationality, or religion. It is an idea—and what an idea it is: That you can come from humble circumstances and do great things. That it doesn't matter where you came from but where you are going.[36]

And here's the thing: it is always easier when those in need have our help along the way. Even

---

36 Speech to RNC, August 8, 2012.

if we are already offering our assistance, there is always more that we can do. We can help ease the plight of the homeless by volunteering at Room at the Inn or by helping to build a home for Habitat for Humanity. We can always do more. We can serve the needs of the hungry by lending a hand at our Thanksgiving Day Boulevard Bolt. We can always do more. Whatever the need—for donations of blood or of clothing, of suitcases or of books—we can always do more. For those who are poor, for those new to our nation's shores—we can always choose to do more. We are Reform Jews, proud of the resonant and relevant voice of our prophetic tradition, which speaks of the finest attributes of our faith: an unrelenting passion for social justice, an unwavering spirit to correct the wrongs of our society and to protect that which is right and those who have rights, unalienable rights granted by our Creator. We—like they—who are created in God's image. We can always do more.

The most sensible way to further our own interests, to find our own freedom, and to glimpse our own happiness is often not to pursue these goals directly, but to look after other people's interests, to help other people be freer from pain, to contribute to their happiness. Ultimately, it is all very simple. We can choose to change our own spirits and, in so doing, we can change the world.[37]

Yes, change is hard. It can be painful. Sometimes even excruciatingly so.

But positive, constructive change is also a necessary component to a healthy and meaningful life. Failing to do so, to adapt and to continue to move forward, would be like wishing for a baby not to grow or asking a child not to thrive or mature. It would be like requesting the ocean to stop moving or hoping that its waves might cease in their attempts to reach the furthest shore.

In the year ahead, may we find the courage to change. May the changes we make change our lives for the good and change the lives of others as well, for the better.

Amen.

---

37   Piero Ferrucci, *The Power of Kindness*, 274.

APPENDIX 3

Dr. Martin Luther King Jr.
"Where Do We Go From Here?"
Speech delivered to the Southern Christian
Leadership Conference, Atlanta
August 16, 1967

Now, in order to answer the question, "Where do we go from here?" which is our theme, we must first honestly recognize where we are now. When the Constitution was written, a strange formula to determine taxes and representation declared that the Negro was 60 percent of a person. Today another curious formula seems to declare he is 50 percent of a person. Of the good things in life, the Negro has approximately one half those of whites. Of the bad things of life, he has twice those of whites. Thus half of all Negroes live in substandard housing. And Negroes have half the income of whites. When we view the negative experiences of life, the Negro has a double share. There are twice as many unemployed. The rate of infant mortality among Negroes is double that of whites and there are twice as many Negroes dying in Vietnam as whites in proportion to their size in the population.

In other spheres, the figures are equally alarming. In elementary schools, Negroes lag one to three years behind whites, and their segregated schools receive substantially less money per student than the white schools. One twentieth as many Negroes as whites attend college. Of employed Negroes, 75 percent hold menial jobs.

This is where we are. Where do we go from here? First, we must massively assert our dignity and worth. We must stand up amidst a system that still oppresses us and develop an unassailable and majestic sense of values. We must no longer be ashamed of being black. The job of arousing manhood within a people that have been taught for so many centuries that they are nobody is not easy.

Depiction of Blackness and Negro Contributions

Even semantics have conspired to make that which is black seem ugly and degrading. In *Roget's Thesaurus* there are 120 synonyms for blackness and at least 60 of them are offensive, as for example, *blot*, *soot*, *grim*, *devil* and *foul*. And there are some 134 synonyms for whiteness and all are favorable, expressed in such words as *purity*, *cleanliness, chastity* and *innocence.* A white lie is better than a black lie. The most degenerate member of a family is a "black sheep." Ossie Davis has suggested that maybe the English language should be reconstructed so that teachers will not be forced to teach the Negro child 60 ways to despise himself, and thereby perpetuate his false sense of inferiority, and the white child 134 ways to adore himself, and thereby perpetuate his false sense of superiority.

The tendency to ignore the Negro's contribution to American life and to strip him of his personhood, is as old as the earliest history hooks and as contemporary as the morning's newspaper. To upset this cultural homicide, the Negro must rise up with an affirmation of his own Olympian manhood. Any movement for the Negro's freedom that overlooks this necessity is only waiting to be buried. As long as the mind is enslaved, the body can never be free. Psychological freedom, a firm sense of self-esteem, is the most powerful weapon against the long night of physical slavery. No Lincolnian Emancipation Proclamation or Johnsonian Civil Rights Bill can totally bring this kind of freedom. The Negro will only be free when he reaches down to the inner depths of his own being and signs with the pen and ink of assertive manhood his own Emancipation Proclamation. And, with a spirit straining toward true self-esteem, the

Negro must boldly throw off the manacles of self-abnegation and say to himself and to the world, "I am somebody. I am a person. I am a man with dignity and honor. I have a rich and noble history. How painful and exploited that history has been. Yes, I was a slave through my foreparents and I am not ashamed of that. I'm ashamed of the people who were so sinful to make me a slave." Yes, we must stand up and say, "I'm black and I'm beautiful," and this self-affirmation is the black man's need, made compelling by the white man's crimes against him.

Basic Challenges

Another basic challenge is to discover how to organize our strength in terms of economic and political power. No one can deny that the Negro is in dire need of this kind of legitimate power. Indeed, one of the great problems that the Negro confronts is his lack of power. From old plantations of the South to newer ghettos of the North, the Negro has been confined to a life of voicelessness and powerlessness. Stripped of the right to make decisions concerning his life and destiny he has been subject to the authoritarian and sometimes whimsical decisions of this white power structure. The plantation and ghetto were created by those who had power, both to confine those who had no power and to perpetuate their powerlessness. The problem of transforming the ghetto, therefore, is a problem of power-confrontation of the forces of power demanding change and the forces of power dedicated to the preserving of the status quo. Now power properly understood is nothing but the ability to achieve purpose. It is the strength required to bring about social, political and economic change. Walter Reuther defined power one day. He said, "Power is the ability of a labor union like the U.A.W. to make the most powerful corporation in the world, General Motors, say 'Yes' when it wants to say 'No.' That's power."

Now a lot of us are preachers, and all of us have our moral convictions and concerns, and so often have problems with power. There is nothing wrong with power if power is used correctly. You see, what happened is that some of our philosophers got off base. And one of the great problems of history is that the concepts of love and power have usually been contrasted as opposites—polar opposites—so that love is identified with a resignation of power, and power with a denial of love.

It was this misinterpretation that caused Nietzsche, who was a philosopher of the will to power, to reject the Christian concept of love. It was this same misinterpretation which induced Christian theologians to reject the Nietzschean philosophy of the will to power in the name of the Christian idea of love. Now, we've got to get this thing right.

What is needed is a realization that power without love is reckless and abusive, and love without power is sentimental and anemic. Power at its best is love implementing the demands of justice, and justice at its best is power correcting everything that stands against love. And this is what we must see as we move on. What has happened is that we have had it wrong and confused in our own country, and this has led Negro Americans in the past to seek their goals through power devoid of love and conscience.

This is leading a few extremists today to advocate for Negroes the same destructive and conscienceless power that they have justly abhorred in whites. It is precisely this collision of immoral power with powerless morality which constitutes the major crisis of our times.

Developing a Program?

We must develop a program that will drive the nation to a guaranteed annual income. Now, early in this century this proposal would have been greeted with ridicule and denunciation, as destructive of initiative and responsibility. At that time economic status was considered the measure of the individual's ability and talents. And, in the thinking of that day, the absence of worldly goods indicated a want of industrious habits and moral fiber. We've come a long way in our understanding of human motivation and of the blind operation of our economic system. Now we realize that dislocations in the market operations of our economy and the prevalence of discrimination thrust people into idleness and bind them in constant or frequent unemployment against their will. Today the poor are less often dismissed, I hope, from our consciences by being branded as inferior or incompetent. We also know that no matter how dynamically the economy develops and expands, it does not eliminate all poverty.

The problem indicates that our emphasis must be twofold. We must create full employment or we must create incomes. People must be made consumers by one method or the other. Once they are placed in this position we need to be concerned that the potential of the individual is not wasted. New forms of work that enhance the social good will have to be devised for those for whom traditional jobs are not available. In 1879 Henry George anticipated this state of affairs when he wrote in Progress and Poverty:

The fact is that the work which improves the condition of mankind, the work which extends knowledge and increases power and enriches literature and elevates thought, is not done to secure a living. It is not the work of slaves driven to their tasks either by the task, by the taskmaster, or by animal necessity. It is the work of men who somehow find a form of work that brings a security for its own sake and a state of society where want is abolished.

Work of this sort could be enormously increased, and we are likely to find that the problems of housing and education, instead of preceding the elimination of poverty, will themselves be affected if poverty is first abolished. The poor transformed into purchasers will do a great deal on their own to alter housing decay. Negroes who have a double disability will have a greater effect on discrimination when they have the additional weapon of cash to use in their struggle.

Beyond these advantages, a host of positive psychological changes inevitably will result from widespread economic security. The dignity of the individual will flourish when the decisions concerning his life are in his own hands, when he has the means to seek self-improvement. Personal conflicts among husbands, wives and children will diminish when the unjust measurement of human worth on the scale of dollars is eliminated.

Now our country can do this. John Kenneth Galbraith said that a guaranteed annual income could be done for about twenty billion dollars a year. And I say to you today, that if our nation can spend thirty-five billion dollars a year to fight an unjust, evil war in Vietnam, and twenty billion dollars to put a man on the moon, it can spend billions of dollars to put God's children on their own two feet right here on earth.

Commitment to Nonviolence

Now, let me say briefly that we must reaffirm our commitment to nonviolence. I want to stress this. The futility of violence in the struggle for racial justice has been tragically etched in all the recent Negro riots. Yesterday, I tried to analyze the riots and deal with their causes. Today I want to give the other side. There is certainly something painfully sad about a riot. One sees screaming youngsters and angry adults fighting hopelessly and aimlessly against impossible odds. And deep down within them, you can even see a desire for self-destruction, a kind of suicidal longing.

Occasionally Negroes contend that the 1965 Watts riot and the other riots in various cities represented effective civil rights action. But those who express this view always end up with stumbling words when asked what concrete gains have been won as a result. At best, the riots have produced a little additional antipoverty money allotted by frightened government officials, and a few water-sprinklers to cool the children of the ghettos. It is something like improving the food in the prison while the people remain securely incarcerated behind bars. Nowhere have the riots won any concrete improvement such as have the organized protest demonstrations. When one tries to pin down advocates of violence as to what acts would be effective, the answers are blatantly illogical. Sometimes they talk of overthrowing racist state and local governments and they talk about guerrilla warfare. They fail to see that no internal revolution has ever succeeded in overthrowing a government by violence unless the government had already lost the allegiance and effective control of its armed forces. Anyone in his right mind knows that this will not happen in the United States. In a violent racial situation, the power structure has the local police, the state troopers, the National Guard and, finally, the Army to call on—all of which are predominantly white. Furthermore, few if any violent revolutions have been successful unless the violent minority had the sympathy and support of the nonresistant majority. Castro may have had only a few Cubans actually fighting with him up in the hills, but he could never have overthrown the Batista regime unless he had the sympathy of the vast majority of Cuban people.

It is perfectly clear that a violent revolution on the part of American blacks would find no sympathy and support from the white population and very little from the majority of the Negroes themselves. This is no time for romantic illusions and empty philosophical debates about freedom. This is a time for action. What is needed is a strategy for change, a tactical program that will bring the Negro into the mainstream of American life as quickly as possible. So far, this has only been offered by the nonviolent movement. Without recognizing this we will end up with solutions that don't solve, answers that don't answer and explanations that don't explain.

And so I say to you today that I still stand by nonviolence. And I am still convinced that it is the most potent weapon available to the Negro in his struggle for justice in this country. And the other thing is that I am concerned about a better world. I'm concerned about justice. I'm concerned about brotherhood. I'm concerned about truth. And when one is concerned about these, he can never advocate violence. For through violence you may murder a murderer but you can't murder. Through violence you may murder a liar but you can't establish truth. Through violence you may murder a hater, but you can't murder hate. Darkness cannot put out darkness. Only light can do that.

And I say to you, I have also decided to stick to love. For I know that love is ultimately the only answer to mankind's problems. And I'm going to talk about it everywhere I go. I know it isn't popular to talk about it in some circles today. I'm not talking about emotional bosh when I talk about love, I'm talking about a strong, demanding love. And I have seen too much hate. I've seen too much hate on the faces of sheriffs in the South. I've seen hate on the faces of too many Klansmen and too many White Citizens Councilors in the South to want to hate myself, because every time I see it, I know that it does something to their faces and their personalities and I say to myself that hate is too great a burden to bear. I have decided to love. If you are seeking the highest good, I think you can find it through love. And the beautiful thing is that we are moving against wrong when we do it, because John was right: God is love. He who hates does not know God, but he who has love has the key that unlocks the door to the meaning of ultimate reality.

I want to say to you as I move to my conclusion, as we talk about "Where do we go from here," that we honestly face the fact that the Movement must address itself to the question of restructuring the whole of American society. There are forty million poor people here. And one day we must ask the question, "Why are there forty million poor people in America?" And when you begin to ask that question, you are raising questions about the economic system, about a broader distribution of wealth. When you ask that question, you begin to question the capitalistic economy. And I'm simply saying that more and more, we've got to begin to ask questions about the whole society. We are called upon to help the discouraged beggars in life's market place. But one day we must come to see that an edifice which produces beggars needs restructuring. It means that questions must be raised. You see, my friends, when you deal with this, you begin to ask the question, "Who owns the oil?" You begin to ask the question, "Who owns the iron ore?" You begin to ask the question, "Why is it that people have to pay water bills in a world that is two thirds water?" These are questions that must be asked.

About Communism

Now, don't think that you have me in a "bind" today. I'm not talking about Communism.

What I'm saying to you this morning is that Communism forgets that life is individual. Capitalism forgets that life is social, and the Kingdom of Brotherhood is found neither in the thesis of Communism nor the antithesis of capitalism but in a higher synthesis. It is found in a higher synthesis that combines the truths of both. Now, when I say question the whole society, it means ultimately coming to see that the problem of racism, the problem of economic exploitation, and the problem of war are all tied together. These are the triple evils that are interrelated.

If you will let me be a preacher just a little bit. One night, a juror came to Jesus and he wanted to know what he could do to be saved. Jesus didn't get bogged down in the kind of isolated approach of what he shouldn't do. Jesus didn't say, "Now Nicodemus, you must stop lying." He didn't say, "Nicodemus, you must stop cheating if you are doing that." He didn't say, "Nicodemus, you must not commit adultery." He didn't say, "Nicodemus, now you must stop drinking liquor if you are doing that excessively." He said something altogether different, because Jesus realized something basic—that if a man will lie, he will steal. And if a man will steal, he will kill. So instead of just getting bogged down in one thing, Jesus looked at him and said, "Nicodemus, you must be born again."

He said, in other words, "Your whole structure must be changed." A nation that will keep people in slavery for 244 years will "thingify" them—make them things. Therefore they will exploit them, and poor people generally, economically. And a nation that will exploit economically will have to have foreign investments and everything else, and will have to use its military might to protect them. All of these problems are tied together. What I am saying today is that we must go from this convention and say, "America, you must be born again!"

Conclusion

So, I conclude by saying again today that we have a task and let us go out with a "divine dissatisfaction." Let us be dissatisfied until America will no longer have a high blood pressure of creeds and an anemia of deeds. Let us be dissatisfied until the tragic walls that separate the outer city of wealth and comfort and the inner city of poverty and despair shall be crushed by the battering rams of the forces of justice. Let us be dissatisfied until those that live on the outskirts of hope are brought into the metropolis of daily security. Let us be dissatisfied until slums are cast into the junk heaps of history, and every family is living in a decent, sanitary home. Let us be dissatisfied until the dark yesterdays of segregated schools will be transformed into bright tomorrows of quality, integrated education. Let us be dissatisfied until integration is not seen as a problem but as an opportunity to participate in the beauty of diversity. Let us be dissatisfied until men and women, however black they may be, will be judged on the basis of the content of their character and not on the basis of the color of their skin. Let us be dissatisfied. Let us be dissatisfied until every state capitol houses a governor who will do justly, who will love mercy and who will walk humbly with his God. Let us be dissatisfied until from every city hall, justice will roll down like waters and righteousness like a mighty stream. Let us be dissatisfied until that day when the lion and the lamb shall lie down together, and every man will sit under his own vine and fig tree and none shall be afraid. Let us be dissatisfied.

And men will recognize that out of one blood God made all men to dwell upon the face of the earth. Let us be dissatisfied until that day when nobody will shout "White Power!"—when nobody will shout "Black Power!"—but everybody will talk about God's power and human power.

I must confess, my friends, the road ahead will not always be smooth. There will still be rocky places of frustration and meandering points of bewilderment. There will be inevitable setbacks here and there. There will be those moments when the buoyancy of hope will be transformed into the fatigue of despair. Our dreams will sometimes be shattered and our ethereal hopes blasted. We may again with tear-drenched eyes have to stand before the bier of some courageous civil-rights worker whose life will be snuffed out by the dastardly acts of bloodthirsty mobs. Difficult and painful as it is, we must walk on in the days ahead with an audacious faith in the future. And as we continue our charted course, we may gain consolation in the words so nobly left by that great black bard who was also a great freedom fighter of yesterday, James Weldon Johnson:

Stony the road we trod,
Bitter the chastening rod
Felt in the days
When hope unborn had died.

Yet with a steady beat,
Have not our weary feet
Come to the place
For which our fathers sighed?

We have come over the way

That with tears hath been watered.
We have come treading our paths
Through the blood of the slaughtered,

Out from the gloomy past,
Till now we stand at last

Where the bright gleam
Of our bright star is cast.

Let this affirmation be our ringing cry. It will give us the courage to face the uncertainties of the future. It will give our tired feet new strength as we continue our forward stride toward the city of freedom. When our days become dreary with low hovering clouds of despair, and when our nights become darker than a thousand midnights, let us remember that there is a creative force in this universe, working to pull down the gigantic mountains of evil, a power that is able to make a way out of no way and transform dark yesterdays into bright tomorrows. Let us realize the arc of the moral universe is long but it bends toward justice.

Let us realize that William Cullen Bryant is right: "Truth crushed to earth will rise again." Let us go out realizing that the Bible is right: "Be not deceived, God is not mocked. Whatsoever a man soweth, that shall he also reap." This is our hope for the future, and with this faith we will be able to sing in some not too distant tomorrow with a cosmic past tense, "We have overcome, we have overcome, deep in my heart, I did believe we would overcome."

INVITATION TO COMMENT

Please know that it would be my pleasure to have an e-mail or note from anyone who takes the time to read my work. I am interested in how you as the reader came upon this book and how you receive the ideas it contains. In other words, how does reading this make you feel? I leave you with my contact information and sincere thanks for sharing your time with my book.

Please send your correspondence to Charles R. Krivcher, ~~P.O. Box 159052, Nashville, TN 37215-9052 or in the alternative~~, via e-mail at krivcherc@bellsouth.net.

Charles R. Krivcher

Made in the USA
Middletown, DE
24 March 2019